Antique Cars & Trucks

You Can Make

By Luc St-Amour

ISBN: 1-896649-03-3

Plans, illustrations, photographs and text in this edition have all been carefully checked and cross-checked. However, due to the variability of construction materials, personal skill, and so on, neither the author nor St-Amour Publishing Inc. assumes any responsibility for any injuries suffered, or damages or other losses incurred that result from the material presented herein. All instructions and plans should be carefully studied and clearly understood before beginning construction.

Printed in Canada

Editor: Rhoda Boyd

St-Amour Publishing Inc.
P.O. Box 74173
Ottawa, Ont.
Canada K1M 2H9

Tel: (613) 834-7520
Fax: (613) 834-7151

IMPORTANT
Notice to parents and readers

The models in this book are designed as display models only, not toys.

There are many small parts that can break easily and be swallowed by a young child!

Check models periodically to ensure that parts have not broken or become loose.

Other books available from St-Amour Publishing Inc.

- *Realistic Construction Models You Can Make*

- *Making Construction Vehicles For Kids*

- *Amazing Vehicles You Can Make*

(see page 127 for details)

Table of Contents

Introduction

This book is for all those who enjoy building wooden models. In this edition you will find clear, easy-to-follow instructions on how to build realistic models of classic cars and trucks.

We have also included details like spoked wheels and doors that open, and suggested various types of wood to add beauty and character to your models.

Two sets of full-sized patterns are provided for each model - a permanent set and a working copy which can be easily transferred onto your work in progress. Clear, concise assembly drawings are also included to guide you through the final stages. For best results, we suggest that you read all instructions before you begin.

Please keep in mind the most important aspect of woodworking - safety!

Best of luck with your projects!

Share your comments and ideas! At St-Amour Publishing Inc. we are always trying to improve. Tell us how you like *Antique Cars & Trucks You Can Make* and what you would like to see in future editions.

_____

_____

_____

_____

_____

_____

_____

_____

_____

_____

_____

_____

_____

Send to: St-Amour Publishing Inc.
                  P.O. Box 74173
                  Ottawa, Ont.
                  Canada K1M 2H9

How to use this book

While there are a lot of different drawings in this book, our approach is very simple. The most important thing to remember is that there are four main steps to making our models.

Step 1

For each model, read the general instructions first. They explain each step thoroughly. Then, cut all materials required by following the accompanying list.

Step 2

When all materials are cut and identified, many parts will already be complete. Some, however, must be finished by following the Parts Drawing section.

Step 3

The rest of the parts can be completed by using the full-sized patterns found in the Appendix. Two sets of full-sized patterns have been provided for each model. Those in the Appendix have been printed on one-sided sheets of paper so they can be easily removed, cut out and attached to the wood. The other set is for reference only and should remain with the book.

Step 4

Once all parts are complete, the Assembly Drawings section provides a step-by-step guide to assembling the model.

The finishing process

When assembling the models, we recommend glue instead of nails or screws. (The only screws that you should use are the ones that hold the hinges on the doors and body.) Wood glues available today are extremely strong and reliable. For that reason, your models should never come apart and will last for years. One of the main advantages of using glue is that materials will not split and the finished product looks great.

Once you complete a model, give it a good sanding using fine grit sandpaper.

Applying the finish

Although there are many types of finish that you can apply to your models, our favorite is a water-based acrylic which is available as a spray. The advantage of using a spray is that it allows you to cover the entire model, even in tight spots.

The finish is applied only after the entire model is assembled and sanded.

Parts that must be purchased

Most of the parts required for the models can be made from scratch, however, there are a few that you must purchase. For example, we recommend that you buy the wheels, wheel pins, headlights, brakelights, hinges, screws and barrels.

Here is a description of the parts that can be purchased.

Spoked Wheels:

2 1/2" diameter x 7/16" thick

The quantity required is specified in the list of materials included with each model.

If you want to get wheels for all 8 models, you will need a total of 38 wheels.

Wheel pins:

1/4" diameter x 1 1/4" long

34 required to make the complete collection.

Headlights:

3/4" outside diameter x 5/8" long

17 required to make all 8 models.

Brakelights (small headlights):

1/2" outside diameter

10 required to make all 8 models.

Hinges & Screws

Hinges: 12 x 16 mm (7/16" x 1/2")
18 required
Matching Screws: #0 x 1/4" long
72 required

Barrels:

1 1/8" diameter x 1 5/8" high
10(+ or -) required

Recommended Tools

Because of the complexity of the models, the use of power tools is a must. They will not only give you the precision needed but will also save you a lot of time.

For some parts, you will be required to make intricate inside cuts. The best tool for this task is the scroll saw.

For sanding purposes, you will need power sanders to save you time and give better results.

The wood needed to make these projects varies in thicknesses which are not standard. This means you will need to use a thickness planer and a bandsaw to re-saw and bring the wood to the specified thickness. (Some of you may have access to these tools at school, from friends or at a store.)

Accessories Needed

- Drill bit set (1/16" to 1/2")
- Flat drill bit set (3/8" to 1")
- Measuring tape
- Combination square
- Sanding drum set
- Wood vice
- Assorted c-clamps
- Awl (Scriber)
- Wood glue
- Wood file
- Pencil and eraser
- 12"ruler (clear recommended)

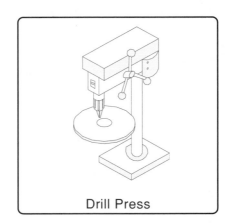

Scroll Saw

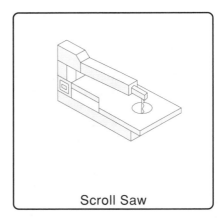

Drill Press

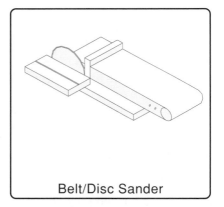

Belt/Disc Sander

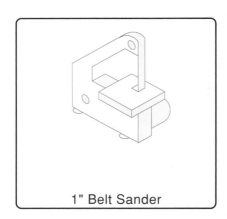

1" Belt Sander

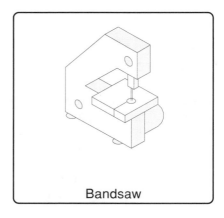

Bandsaw

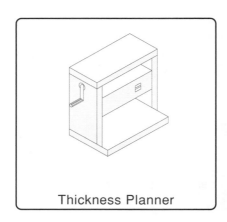

Thickness Planner

Recommended Jig

Some of the parts found in our models are very narrow (e.g. the top sections on the rumble seats). To make these parts, we recommend that you do all the shaping and finishing by using a 1" belt sander, as shown on the previous page. To keep this operation safe, we also recommend that you make the following jig (clamping device). This will allow you to hold the material while finishing it. It would be unsafe to use your hands to hold the piece while sanding and the results may not be satisfactory.

Materials required

1 piece of threaded rod 5/16' dia. x 3 3/4" long
2 5/16" washers
2 5/16" nut
1 5/16" wing nut
1 piece of maple dowel 1/2" dia. x 4 3/4" long
   Maple to make parts A,B and C.

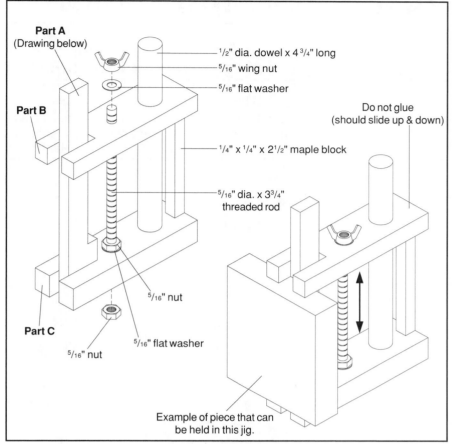

Part A
(Drawing below)

Part B

Part C

1/2" dia. dowel x 4 3/4" long
5/16" wing nut
5/16" flat washer
Do not glue
(should slide up & down)
1/4" x 1/4" x 2 1/2" maple block
5/16" dia. x 3 3/4" threaded rod
5/16" nut
5/16" flat washer
5/16" nut

Example of piece that can be held in this jig.

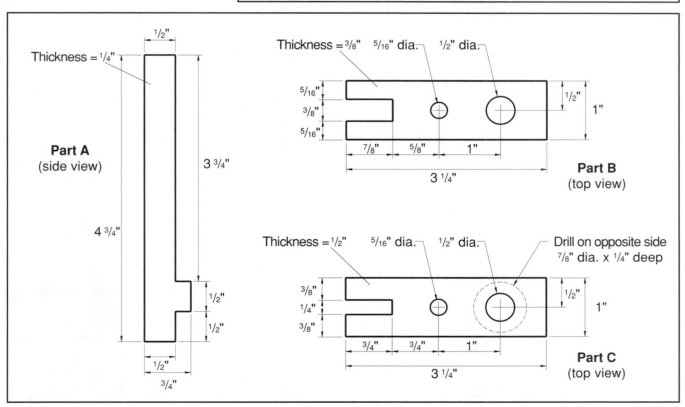

Thickness = 1/4"
1/2"

Part A
(side view)

3 3/4"
4 3/4"
1/2"
1/2"
1/2"
3/4"

Thickness = 3/8"   5/16" dia.   1/2" dia.
5/16"
3/8"
5/16"
1/2"
1"
7/8"   5/8"   1"
3 1/4"

Part B
(top view)

Thickness = 1/2"   5/16" dia.   1/2" dia.   Drill on opposite side 7/8" dia. x 1/4" deep
3/8"
1/4"
3/8"
1/2"
1"
3/4"   3/4"   1"
3 1/4"

Part C
(top view)

Additional Information

Steps for making openings in fenders and drilling holes for headlights

The following step applies only to the models that have a spare wheel on the side of their hood. Models with that feature will require you to cut out an opening in one of the fenders by using your scroll saw. The technique is explained below. Please note: On most of the fender patterns, you will see another guideline positioned at the front of the fender. Transfer this guideline, then drill a 1/8" diameter hole in the centre for headlights.

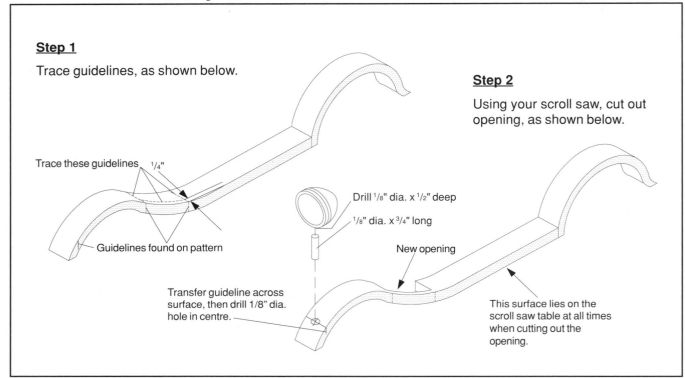

Step 1

Trace guidelines, as shown below.

Step 2

Using your scroll saw, cut out opening, as shown below.

Trace these guidelines   1/4"

Guidelines found on pattern

Drill 1/8" dia. x 1/2" deep

1/8" dia. x 3/4" long

New opening

Transfer guideline across surface, then drill 1/8" dia. hole in centre.

This surface lies on the scroll saw table at all times when cutting out the opening.

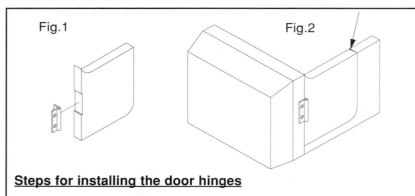

Fig.1   Fig.2

Steps for installing the door hinges

Step 1: Cut an opening centered on the door, as shown in Figure 1. (Note: the opening should match the size of the hinge.)

Step 2: Install door onto body frame, as shown in Figure 2. (Note: you will probably need to sand the face of the door to allow it to close properly. The surface that must be sanded is shown with an arrow.)

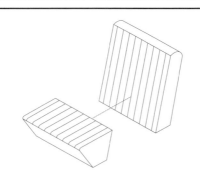

Step to make your seats realistic

Once you have completed the two sections required for a complete seat, you can cut grooves 1/4" apart on the seat surfaces. This step must be done before glueing parts together.

1910 Classic Sedan

Step 1

Start by cutting materials needed using the List of Materials on pages 11 and 12. **Pay attention to the rough and finished size, and identify parts as they are cut.**

Step 2

Parts A1 to A3 are already complete. Parts A4 to A6 will need a few more steps. See the Parts Drawing section on page 13 for more details.

Step 3

Parts A7 to A22 require removing the Full-Sized Patterns sheet found on pages 95 and 97 of the Appendix. Cut out the patterns, leaving approximately $1/16$" all around, and place on the proper piece of wood. Patterns can be secured to the wood using either spray adhesive or rubber cement. If using the latter, cut and sand the part first to finished size. If drilling is required, mark the hole by inserting an awl or nail through the pattern into the wood. Remove the pattern before drilling. (Note: arrows found on patterns indicate grain direction.)

You should have no trouble determining which surface to attach most of the patterns. Some parts, however, can be confusing since the pattern could fit on more than one surface. The drawings in Figure 1 indicate exactly which surface to use. Please note: After completing these parts, the windshield, part A10 has to be sanded on an angle. See page 18 for more information.

Step 4

Follow the Assembly Drawings on pages 16 and 17 to complete your model.

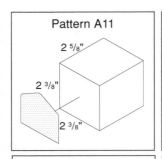
Pattern A11

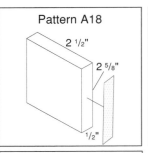
Pattern A18

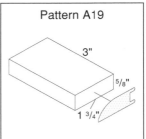
Pattern A19

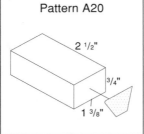
Pattern A20

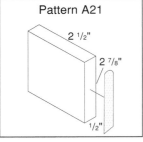
Pattern A21

Fig. 1

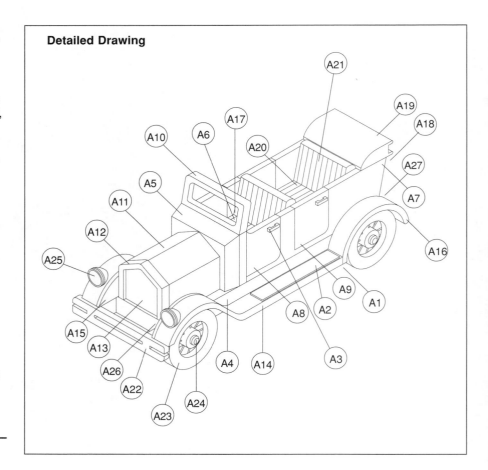
Detailed Drawing

Part	Description	Qty.	T	W	L	Material	*
A1	Axle Blocks	2	1/2"	3/4"	3"	Maple	F
A2	Floor Boards	2	1/16"	5/8"	4"	Mahogony	F
A3	Door Handles	4	1/8"	1/8"	1/2"	Maple	F
A4	Main Frame	1	3/4"	3"	11 5/8"	Maple	F
A5	Cove	1	1"	3"	2 3/8"	Mahogony	F
A6	Steering Column	1	1/4" dia.		1 1/2"	Maple Dowel	F
A7	Body Sides	2	1/4"	2 7/16"	7 1/2"	Mahogony	R
A8	Front Doors	2	1/4"	2"	2 3/8"	Mahogony	R
A9	Rear Doors	2	1/4"	2"	2 1/8"	Mahogony	R
A10	Windshield	1	1/4"	3 1/4"	1 3/4"	Oak	R
A11	Hood	1	2 3/8"	2 3/8"	2 5/8"	Mahogony	F
A12	Grill Cover	1	3/8"	2 1/2"	2 3/8"	Pine	R
A13	Grill	1	1/4"	2"	2"	Oak	R
A14	Front Fenders	2	3/4"	1 7/8"	9 1/4"	Pine	R
A15	Fender - Inside Covers	2	1/8"	1 1/8"	3 3/8"	Pine	R
A16	Rear Fenders	2	3/4"	1 7/8"	3 3/8"	Pine	R
A17	Steering Wheel	1	1/8"	1 3/8"	1 3/8"	Maple	R
A18	Body - End Cover	1	1/2"	2 1/2"	2 5/8"	Mahogony	F
A19	Folded Rag Top	1	5/8"	3"	1 3/4"	Pine	F
A20	Seats - Lower Section	2	3/4"	2 1/2"	1 3/8"	Oak	R

(continued on next page)

Part	Description	Qty.	T	W	L	Material	*
A21	Seat - Top Sections	2	1/2"	2 1/2"	2 7/8"	Oak	R
A22	Front Bumper	1	1/4"	1"	4 3/4"	Oak	R
A23	Wheels	5	2 1/2" dia. x 7/16" thick			Hard Wood	$
A24	Wheel Pins	5	1/4" dia. x 1 1/4" long			Hard Wood	$
A25	Headlights	2	3/4" dia. x 5/8" long			Hard Wood	$
A26	Small Headlights	2	1/2" dia. x 1/2" long			Hard Wood	$
A27	Hinges	4	12 x 16mm (7/16" x 1/2")			Brass Plated	$
A28	Hinge Screws	16	#0 x 1/4" long			Brass	$

T = Thickness	R = Rough size
W = Width	F = Finished size
L = Length	$ = Parts to be purchased

Instructions for cutting and shaping materials

R = Rough size

The material is cut oversized so you have ample room to apply the patterns on the surface. Sanding is not required at this point.

F = Finished size

Carefully cut and sand materials to specified dimensions, making sure surfaces are square and parallel.

**A4
Main Frame**

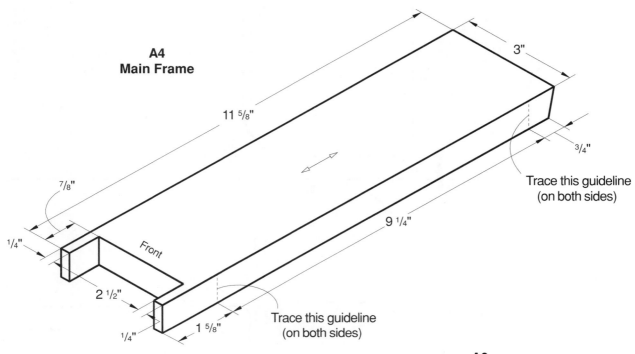

11 5/8"

3"

3/4"

Trace this guideline
(on both sides)

9 1/4"

7/8"

1/4"

Front

2 1/2"

1/4"

1 5/8"

Trace this guideline
(on both sides)

**A6
Steering Column**

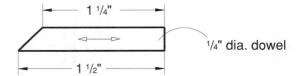

1 1/4"

1/4" dia. dowel

1 1/2"

**A5
Cove**

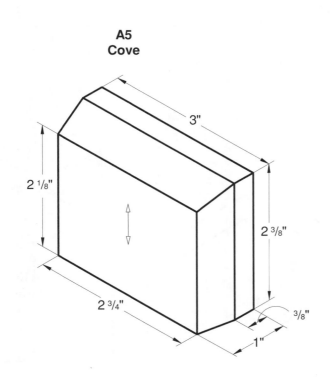

3"

2 1/8"

2 3/8"

2 3/4"

3/8"

1"

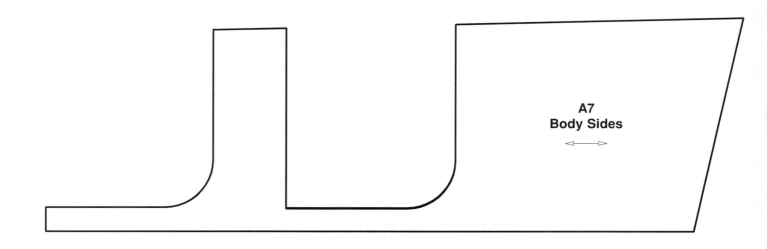

A7
Body Sides

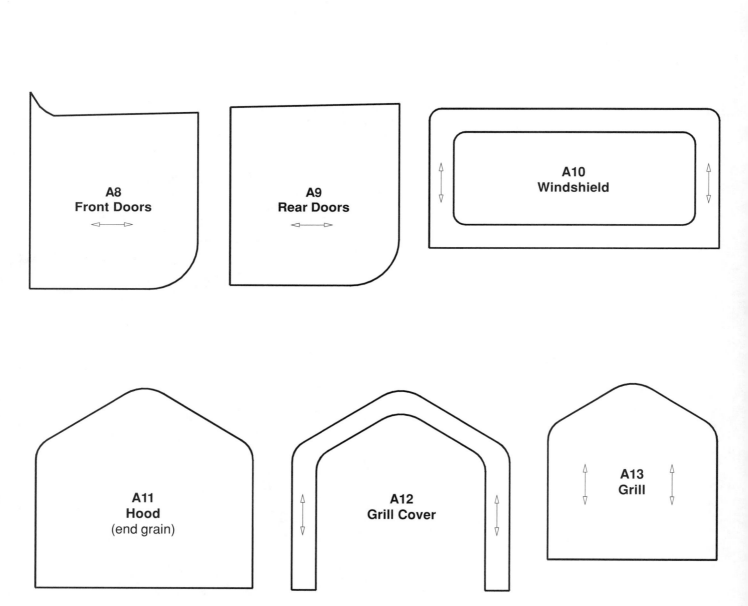

A8
Front Doors

A9
Rear Doors

A10
Windshield

A11
Hood
(end grain)

A12
Grill Cover

A13
Grill

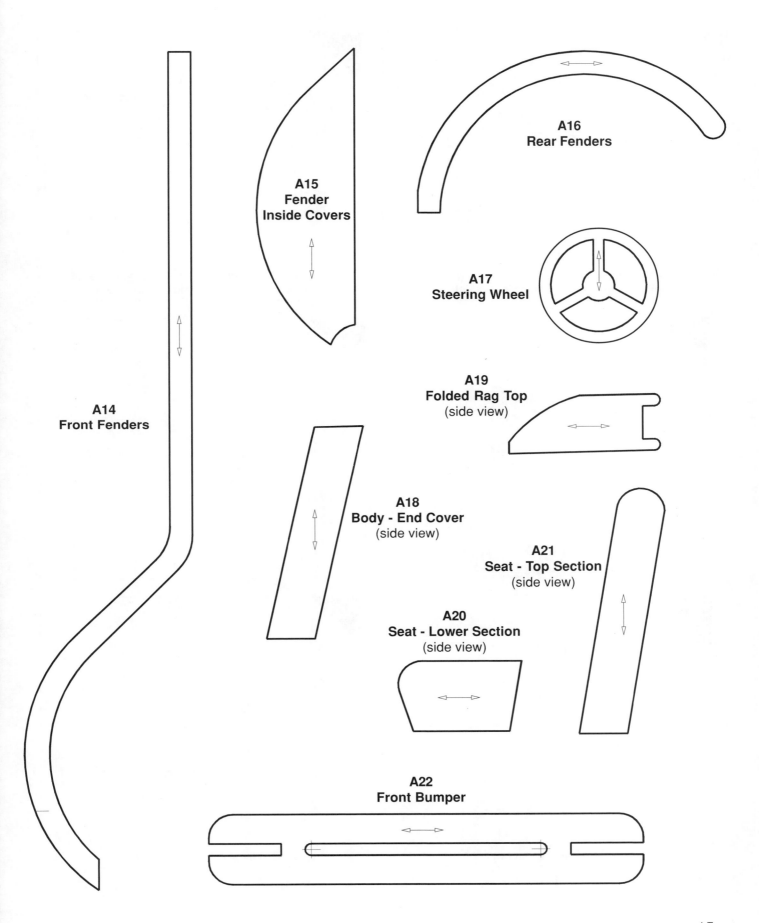

A16
Rear Fenders

A15
Fender
Inside Covers

A17
Steering Wheel

A19
Folded Rag Top
(side view)

A14
Front Fenders

A18
Body - End Cover
(side view)

A21
Seat - Top Section
(side view)

A20
Seat - Lower Section
(side view)

A22
Front Bumper

1

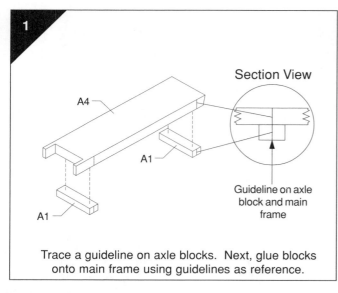

Section View

A4

A1

A1

Guideline on axle block and main frame

Trace a guideline on axle blocks. Next, glue blocks onto main frame using guidelines as reference.

2

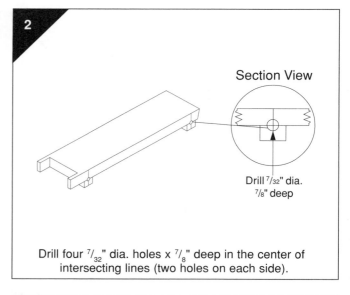

Section View

Drill $^7/_{32}$" dia. $^7/_8$" deep

Drill four $^7/_{32}$" dia. holes x $^7/_8$" deep in the center of intersecting lines (two holes on each side).

3

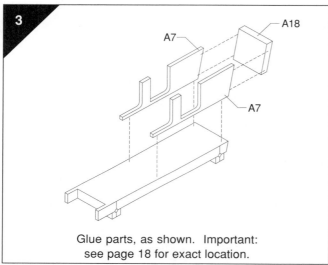

A18

A7

A7

Glue parts, as shown. Important: see page 18 for exact location.

4

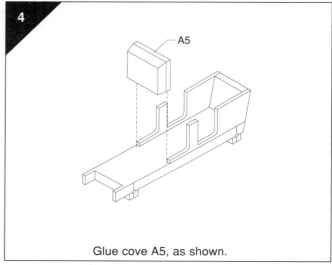

A5

Glue cove A5, as shown.

5

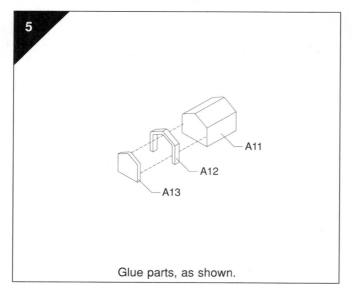

A11

A12

A13

Glue parts, as shown.

6

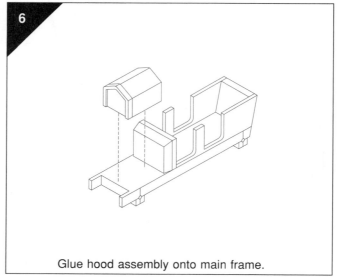

Glue hood assembly onto main frame.

7

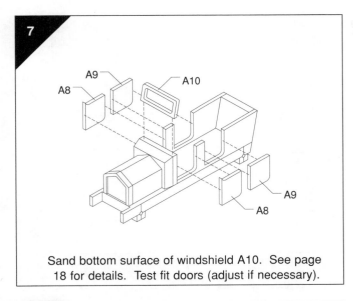

Sand bottom surface of windshield A10. See page 18 for details. Test fit doors (adjust if necessary).

8

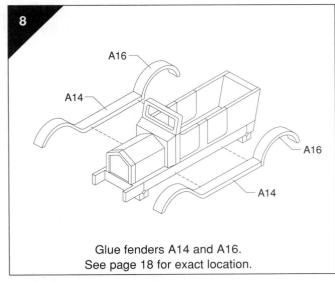

Glue fenders A14 and A16. See page 18 for exact location.

9

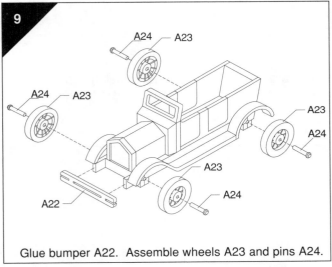

Glue bumper A22. Assemble wheels A23 and pins A24.

10

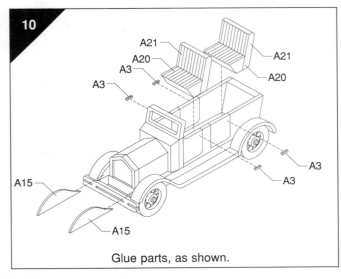

Glue parts, as shown.

11

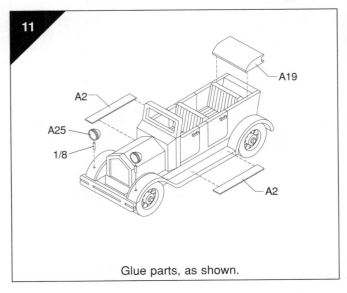

Glue parts, as shown.

12

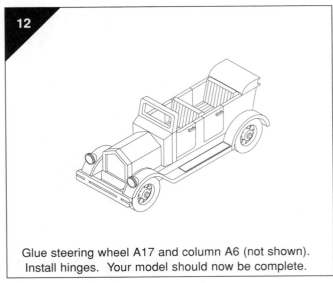

Glue steering wheel A17 and column A6 (not shown). Install hinges. Your model should now be complete.

The section drawing below shows where to glue body
sides A7, front fenders A14 and rear fenders A16.

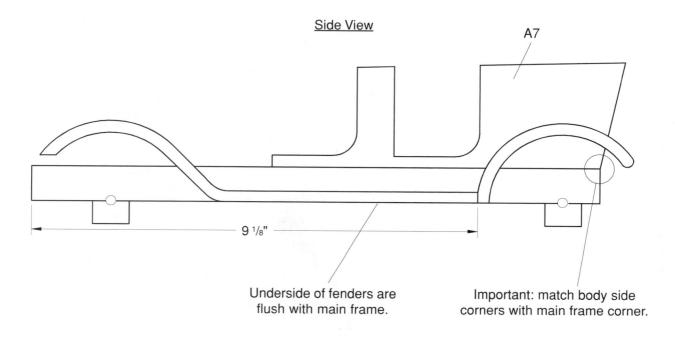

Side View

A7

9 ¹/₈"

Underside of fenders are
flush with main frame.

Important: match body side
corners with main frame corner.

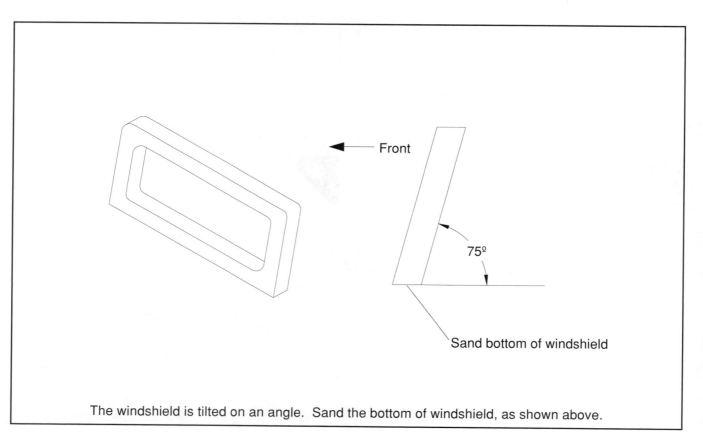

Front

75º

Sand bottom of windshield

The windshield is tilted on an angle. Sand the bottom of windshield, as shown above.

Mid-1920s Fire Truck

Step 1

Start by cutting materials needed using the List of Materials on pages 21 and 22. **Pay attention to the rough and finished size, and identify parts as they are cut.**

Step 2

Parts B1 to B9 are already complete. Parts B10 to B20 will need a few more steps. See the Parts Drawing section on pages 23 and 24 for more details.

Step 3

Parts B21 to B35 require removing the Full-Sized Patterns sheet found on pages 99 and 101 of the Appendix. Cut out the patterns, leaving approximately $1/16$" all around, and place on the proper piece of wood. Patterns can be secured to the wood using either spray adhesive or rubber cement. If using the latter, cut and sand the part first to finished size. If drilling is required, mark the hole by inserting an awl or nail through the pattern into the wood. Remove the pattern before drilling. (Note: arrows found on patterns indicate grain direction.)

You should have no trouble determining which surface to attach most of the patterns. Some parts, however, can be confusing since the pattern could fit on more than one surface. The drawings in Figure 1 indicate exactly which surface to use.

Step 4

Follow the Assembly Drawings on pages 27, 28 and 29 to complete your model.

Please note: the rubber hose used is actually a piece of windshield-washer hose from a real car.

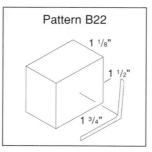

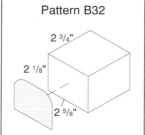

Fig. 1

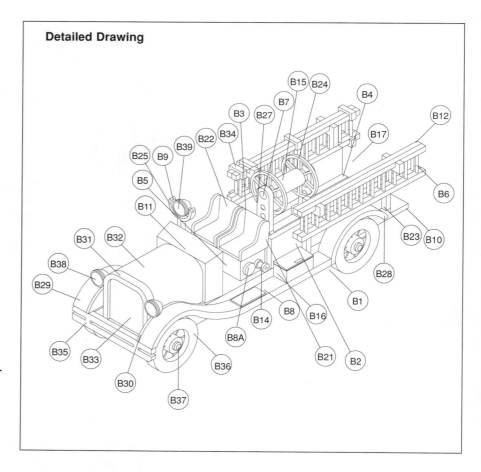

Detailed Drawing

Part	Description	Qty.	T	W	L	Material	*
B1	Axle Blocks	2	1/2"	3/4"	3"	Maple	F
B2	Body Sides	2	1/4"	1 1/2"	6 3/4"	Mahogony	F
B3	Body - End Piece	1	1/4"	1 1/2"	2 1/2"	Mahogony	F
B4	Floor Planks	7	1/8"	3/8"	6 1/2"	Oak	F
B5	Seat Frame	1	1 1/8"	2 1/2"	1 3/8"	Mahogony	F
B6	Ladder Posts	44	1/8" dia.		1 1/4"	Maple Dowel	F
B7	Hose Reel Shaft	1	3/8" dia.		2 3/8"	Maple Dowel	F
B8	Floor Boards	2	1/16"	5/8"	1 3/8"	Mahogony	F
B8A	Pressure Dial	1	1/8"	1/2" dia.		Maple Dowel	F
B8B	Radiator Cap	1	1/8"	3/16"	5/16"	Mahogony	F
B9	Flood Light Pivot Pin	1	1/8" dia.		1 1/4"	Maple Dowel	F
B10	Main Frame	1	3/4"	3"	15"	Maple	F
B11	Cove	1	3/4"	3"	2 1/4"	Mahogony	F
B12	Ladder Sides	8	1/4"	1/4"	7"	Maple	F
B13	Steering Column	1	1/4" dia.		1 7/8"	Maple Dowel	F
B14	Hose Connector	1	3/8" dia.		1 1/2"	Maple Dowel	F
B15	Hose Reel Drum	1	3/4" dia.		1 1/2"	Maple Dowel	F
B16	Storage Boxes	2	3/4"	3/4"	1 1/2"	Oak	F
B17	Safety Bars	2	1/8" dia.		2 5/16"	Maple Dowel	F
B18	Flood Light Cap	1	1/8"	1/4" dia.		Maple Dowel	F
B18A	Flood Light Shaft	1	1/8" dia.		1 1/2"	Maple Dowel	F
B19	Flood Light Bracket	1	1/4"	3/8"	3/4"	Maple	F
B20	Hose Sprayer	1	3/8" dia.		1 1/2"	Maple Dowel	R

(continued on next page)

T = Thickness	**R** = Rough size
W = Width	**F** = Finished size
L = Length	**$** = Parts to be purchased

Part	Description	Qty.	T	W	L	Material	*
B21	Seat Sides	4	1/8"	1 3/4"	1 1/2"	Oak	R
B22	Seat - Centre Pieces	2	1 1/8"	1 1/2"	1 3/4"	Oak	R
B23	Ladder Supports	4	1/4"	1 1/4"	2 7/8"	Maple	R
B24	Hose Reel Sides	2	1/8"	2 1/4"	2 1/4"	Maple	R
B25	Flood Light Frame	1	1/4"	1 1/2"	1 1/2"	Maple	R
B26	Steering Wheel	1	1/8"	1 3/8"	1 3/8"	Maple	R
B27	Main Supports - Hose Reel	2	1/4"	1 5/8"	3"	Maple	R
B28	Rear Fenders	2	3/4"	2"	3 3/8"	Pine	R
B29	Front Fenders	2	3/4"	2"	10 1/4"	Pine	R
B30	Fender - Inside Covers	2	1/8"	1 1/4"	3 3/8"	Pine	R
B31	Grill Cover	1	3/8"	2 3/4"	3"	Pine	R
B32	Hood	1	2 1/8"	2 5/8"	2 3/4"	Mahogony	F
B33	Grill	1	1/4"	2 1/4"	2 1/2"	Oak	R
B34	Ladder - Slide Brackets	8	1/4"	1/2"	7/8"	Maple	R
B35	Front Bumper	1	1/4"	1"	4 3/4"	Oak	R
B36	Wheels	4	2 1/2" dia. x 7/16" thick			Hard Wood	$
B37	Wheel Pins	4	1/4" dia. x 1 1/4" long			Hard Wood	$
B38	Headlights	2	3/4" dia. x 5/8" long			Hard Wood	$
B39	Floodlight	1	3/4" dia. x 5/8" long			Hard Wood	$
B40	Hose	1	1/4" dia. x 24" long (hose)			Rubber	$

Instructions for cutting and shaping materials

R = Rough size The material is cut oversized so you have ample room to apply the patterns on the surface. Sanding is not required at this point.

F = Finished size Carefully cut and sand materials to specified dimensions, making sure surfaces are square and parallel.

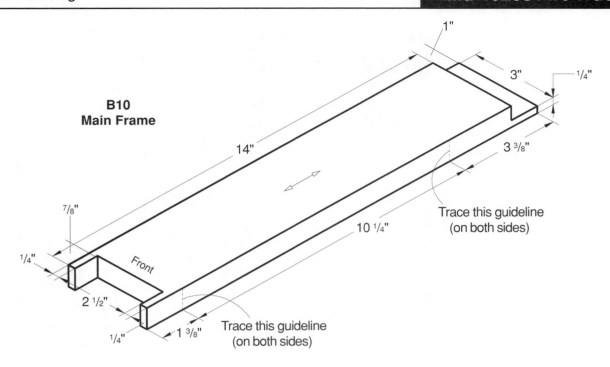

**B10
Main Frame**

1"

3"

1/4"

14"

3 3/8"

Trace this guideline
(on both sides)

7/8"

10 1/4"

1/4"

Front

2 1/2"

1/4"

1 3/8"

Trace this guideline
(on both sides)

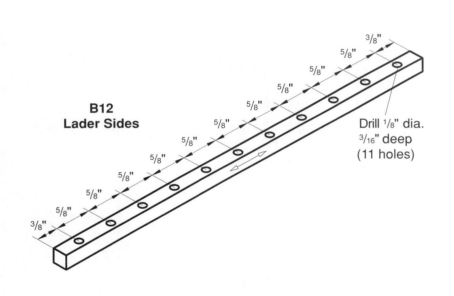

**B12
Lader Sides**

3/8"

5/8"

5/8"

5/8"

5/8"

5/8"

5/8"

5/8"

5/8"

5/8"

5/8"

5/8"

3/8"

Drill 1/8" dia.
3/16" deep
(11 holes)

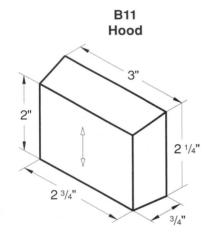

**B11
Hood**

3"

2"

2 1/4"

2 3/4"

3/4"

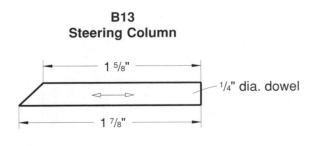

**B13
Steering Column**

1 5/8"

1/4" dia. dowel

1 7/8"

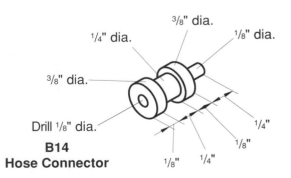

3/8" dia.

1/4" dia.

1/8" dia.

3/8" dia.

Drill 1/8" dia.

**B14
Hose Connector**

1/4"

1/8"

1/8"

1/4"

B15
Hose Reel Drum

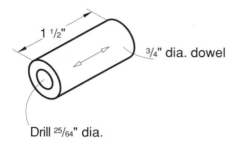

1 1/2"

3/4" dia. dowel

Drill 25/64" dia.

B16
Storage Box

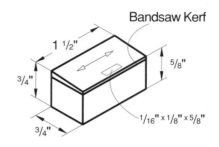

Bandsaw Kerf

1 1/2"

5/8"

3/4"

3/4"

1/16" x 1/8" x 5/8"

B17
Safety Bars

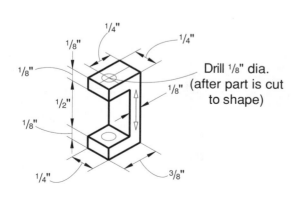

2 5/16"

2"

1/8" dia. dowel

B18
Flood Light Cap

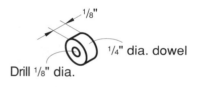

1/8"

1/4" dia. dowel

Drill 1/8" dia.

B19
Flood Light Bracket

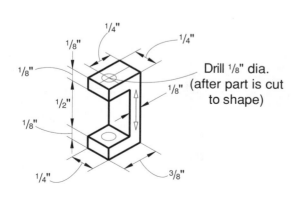

1/4"

1/8"

1/8"

1/4"

1/8"

1/2"

1/8"

Drill 1/8" dia.
(after part is cut
to shape)

1/8"

1/4"

3/8"

B20
Hose Sprayer

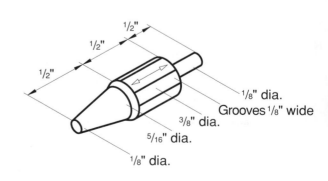

1/2"

1/2"

1/2"

1/8" dia.

Grooves 1/8" wide

3/8" dia.

5/16" dia.

1/8" dia.

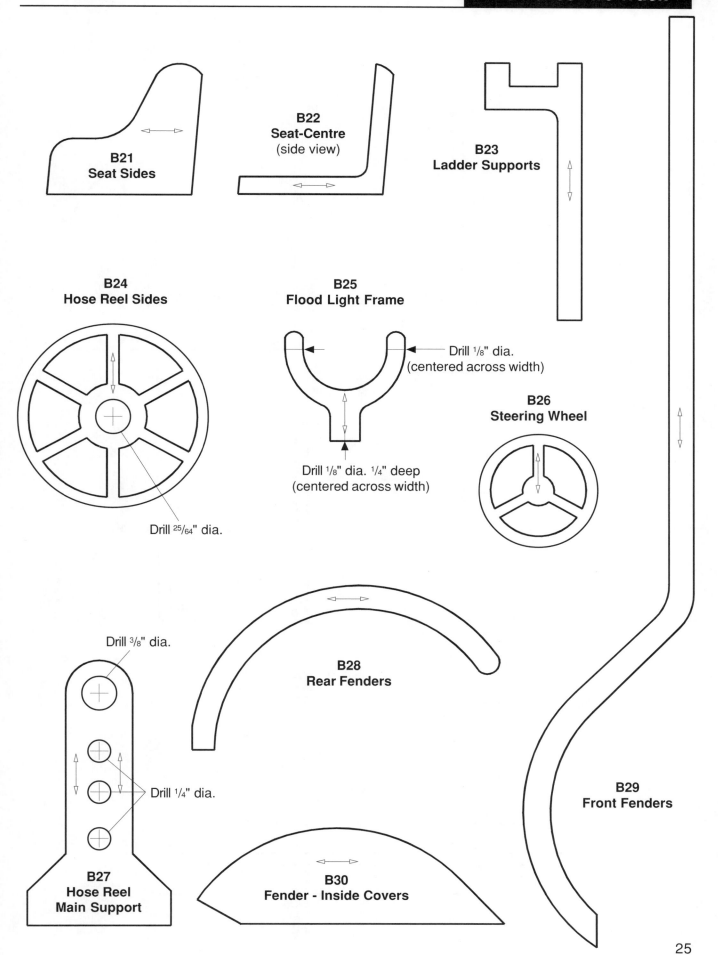

B21
Seat Sides

B22
Seat-Centre
(side view)

B23
Ladder Supports

B24
Hose Reel Sides

B25
Flood Light Frame

Drill $\frac{1}{8}$" dia.
(centered across width)

Drill $\frac{1}{8}$" dia. $\frac{1}{4}$" deep
(centered across width)

B26
Steering Wheel

Drill $\frac{25}{64}$" dia.

B28
Rear Fenders

Drill $\frac{3}{8}$" dia.

Drill $\frac{1}{4}$" dia.

B29
Front Fenders

B27
Hose Reel
Main Support

B30
Fender - Inside Covers

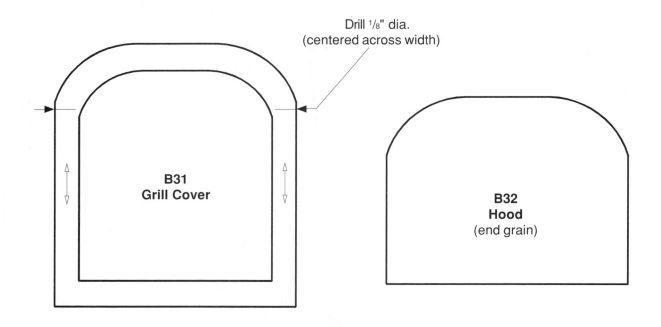

Drill ⅛" dia.
(centered across width)

**B31
Grill Cover**

**B32
Hood**
(end grain)

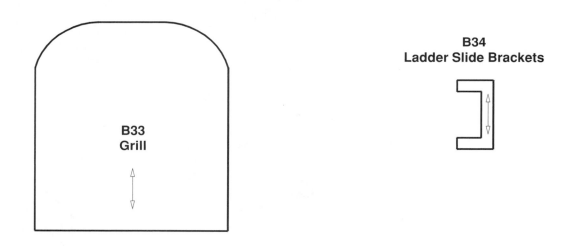

**B33
Grill**

**B34
Ladder Slide Brackets**

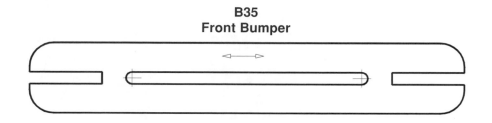

**B35
Front Bumper**

1

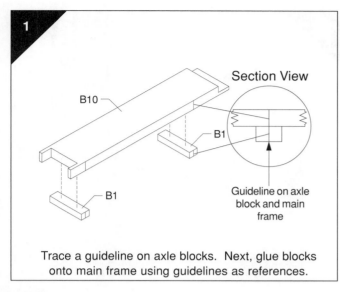

Section View

B10

B1

Guideline on axle block and main frame

B1

Trace a guideline on axle blocks. Next, glue blocks onto main frame using guidelines as references.

2

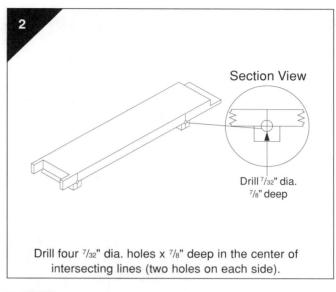

Section View

Drill $7/32$" dia. $7/8$" deep

Drill four $7/32$" dia. holes x $7/8$" deep in the center of intersecting lines (two holes on each side).

3

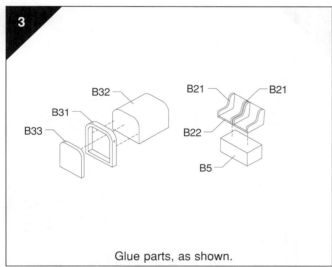

B32

B31

B33

B21

B22

B21

B5

Glue parts, as shown.

4

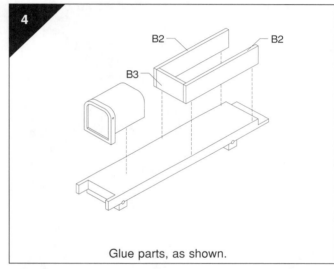

B2

B2

B3

Glue parts, as shown.

5

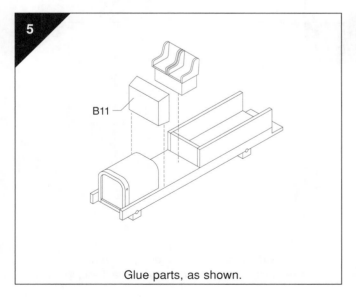

B11

Glue parts, as shown.

6

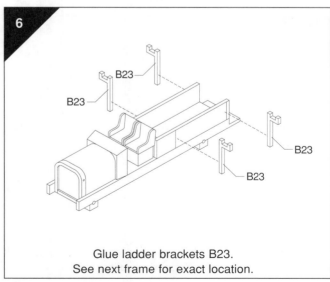

B23

B23

B23

B23

Glue ladder brackets B23.
See next frame for exact location.

7

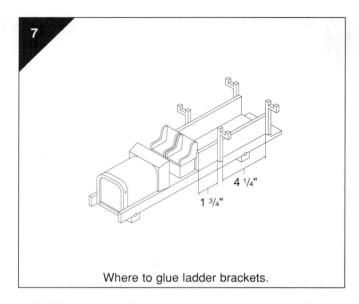

1 3/4" 4 1/4"

Where to glue ladder brackets.

8

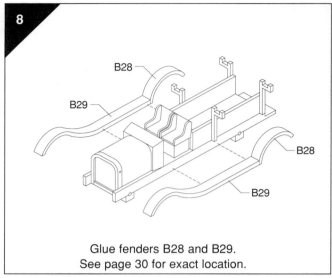

B28
B29
B28
B29

Glue fenders B28 and B29.
See page 30 for exact location.

9

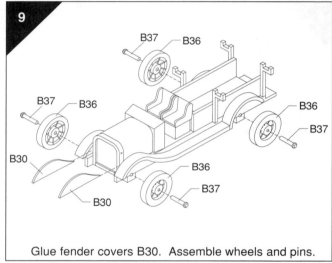

B37 B36
B37 B36
B36
B37
B30
B36
B30
B37

Glue fender covers B30. Assemble wheels and pins.

10

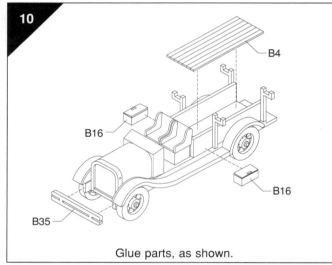

B4
B16
B16
B35

Glue parts, as shown.

11

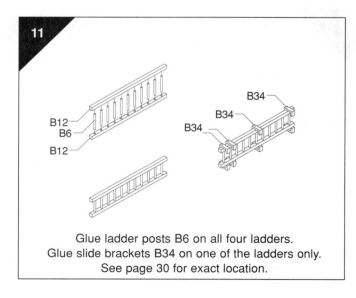

B12
B6
B12
B34
B34
B34

Glue ladder posts B6 on all four ladders.
Glue slide brackets B34 on one of the ladders only.
See page 30 for exact location.

12

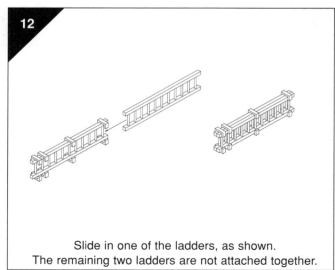

Slide in one of the ladders, as shown.
The remaining two ladders are not attached together.

13

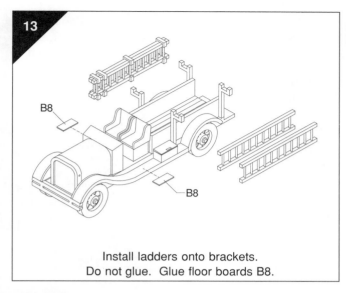

Install ladders onto brackets.
Do not glue. Glue floor boards B8.

14

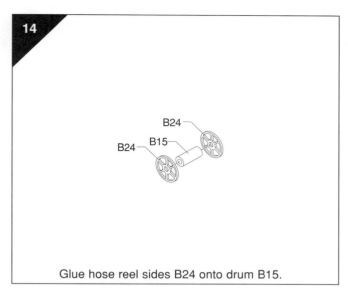

Glue hose reel sides B24 onto drum B15.

15

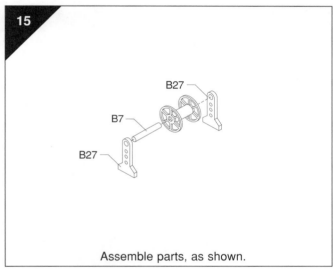

Assemble parts, as shown.

16

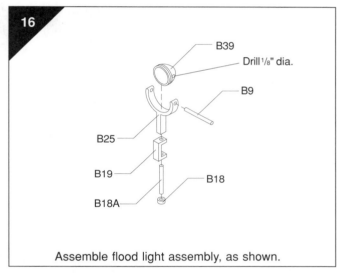

Assemble flood light assembly, as shown.

17

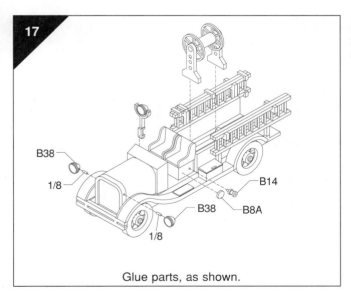

Glue parts, as shown.

18

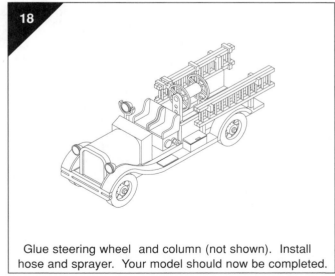

Glue steering wheel and column (not shown). Install
hose and sprayer. Your model should now be completed.

The section drawing below shows where to glue
rear fenders B28 and front fenders B29.

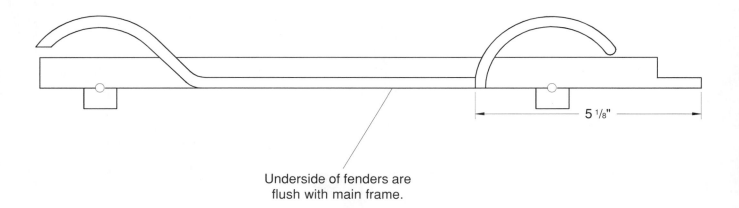

5 1/8"

Underside of fenders are
flush with main frame.

The drawing below shows where to
glue ladder slide brackets B34.

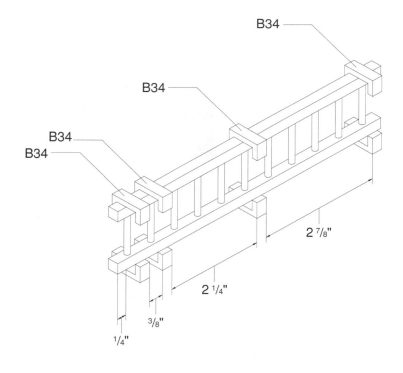

B34

B34

B34

B34

2 7/8"

2 1/4"

3/8"

1/4"

Late-1920s Sport Sedan

Late-1920s Sport Sedan

Step 1

Start by cutting materials needed using the List of Materials on page 33 and 34. **Pay attention to the rough and finished size, and identify parts as they are cut.**

Step 2

Parts C1 to C4A are already completed. Parts C5 and C6 will need a few more steps. See the Parts Drawing section on page 35 for more details.

Step 3

Parts C7 to C22 require removing the Full-Sized Patterns sheet found on pages 103 and 105 of the Appendix. Cut out the patterns, leaving approximately $1/16$" all around, and place on the proper piece of wood. Patterns can be secured to the wood using either spray adhesive or rubber cement. If using the latter, cut and sand the part first to finished size. If drilling is required, mark the hole by inserting an awl or nail through the pattern into the wood. Remove the pattern before drilling. (Note: arrows found on patterns indicate grain direction.)

You should have no trouble determining which surface to attach most of the patterns. Some parts, however, can be confusing since the pattern could fit on more than one surface. The drawings in Figure 1 indicate exactly which surface to attach the patterns for these parts. Please note: for pattern C20, you must cut out an opening for the spare wheel. Follow the instruction on page 8 to see how this step is done.

Step 4

Follow the Assembly Drawings on pages 38 and 39 to complete your model.

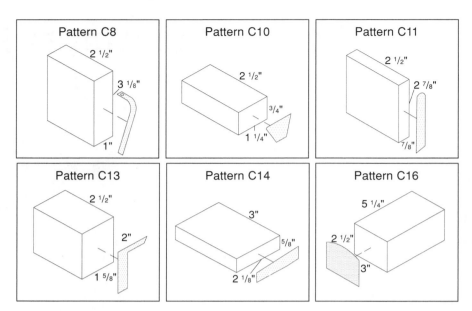

Fig. 1

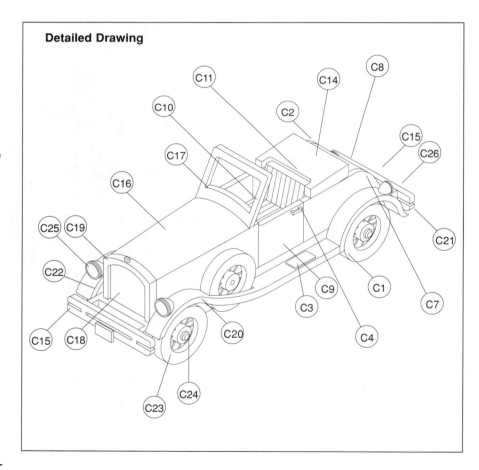

Detailed Drawing

Part	Description	Qty.	T	W	L	Material	*
C1	Axle Blocks	2	1/2"	3/4"	3"	Maple	F
C2	Pivot Pins	2	1/8" dia.		3/8"	Maple Dowel	F
C3	Floor Boards	2	1/16"	5/8"	1 1/8"	Mahogony	F
C4	Door Handles	2	1/8"	1/8"	1/2"	Maple	F
C4A	Licence Plates	2	1/8"	1/2"	7/8"	Mahogony	F
C5	Main Frame	1	3/4"	3"	13 3/4"	Maple	F
C6	Steering Column	1	1/4" dia.		1 1/2"	Maple Dowel	F
C7	Body Sides	2	1/4"	2 1/8"	4 3/4"	Mahogony	R
C8	Trunk	1	1"	2 1/2"	3 1/8"	Mahogony	F
C9	Doors	2	1/4"	2 1/4"	2 5/8"	Mahogony	R
C10	Seat - Lower Section	1	3/4"	2 1/2"	1 1/4"	Pine	R
C11	Seat - Top Section	1	7/8"	2 1/2"	2 7/8"	Pine	R
C12	Steering Wheel	1	1/8"	1 3/8"	1 3/8"	Maple	R
C13	Trunk Divider	1	2"	2 1/2"	1 5/8"	Mahogony	F
C14	Folded Rag Top	1	5/8"	3"	2 1/8"	Pine	F
C15	Bumpers	2	1/4"	1"	4 3/4"	Oak	R
C16	Hood	1	2 1/2"	3"	5 1/4"	Mahogony	F
C17	Windshield	1	1/4"	3 1/4"	2 1/4"	Mahogony	R
C18	Grill	1	1/4"	2 1/4"	2 1/4"	Oak	R
C19	Grill Cover	1	3/8"	2 3/4"	2 3/8"	Pine	R

(continued on next page)

Part	Description	Qty.	T	W	L	Material	*
C20	Front Fenders	2	3/4"	1 7/8"	9 3/4"	Pine	R
C21	Rear Fenders	2	3/4"	2"	4"	Pine	R
C22	Fender - Inside Covers	2	1/8"	1 1/4"	4 3/8"	Pine	R
C23	Wheels	5	2 1/2" dia. x 7/16" thick			Hard Wood	$
C24	Wheel Pins	4	1/4" dia. x 1 1/4" long			Hard Wood	$
C25	Headlights	2	3/4" dia. x 5/8" long			Hard Wood	$
C26	Brake Lights	2	1/2" dia. x 1/2" long			Hard Wood	$
C27	Hinges	2	12 x 16mm (7/16" x 1/2")			Brass Plated	$
C28	Hinges Screws	8	#0 x 1/4" long			Brass	$

T = Thickness **W** = Width **L** = Length	**R** = Rough size **F** = Finished size **$** = Parts to be purchased

Instructions for cutting and shaping materials

R = Rough size

The material is cut oversized so you have ample room to apply the patterns on the surface. Sanding is not required at this point.

F = Finished size

Carefully cut and sand materials to specified dimensions, making sure surfaces are square and parallel.

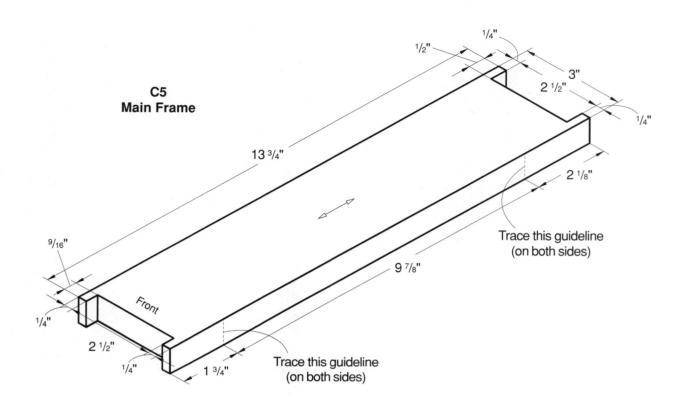

**C5
Main Frame**

13 ³/₄"

1/4"

1/2"

3"

2 1/2"

1/4"

2 1/8"

Trace this guideline
(on both sides)

9 ⁷/₈"

9/16"

Front

1/4"

2 1/2"

1/4"

1 ³/₄"

Trace this guideline
(on both sides)

**C6
Steering Column**

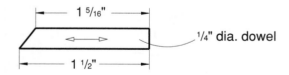

1 ⁵/₁₆"

1 ¹/₂"

¹/₄" dia. dowel

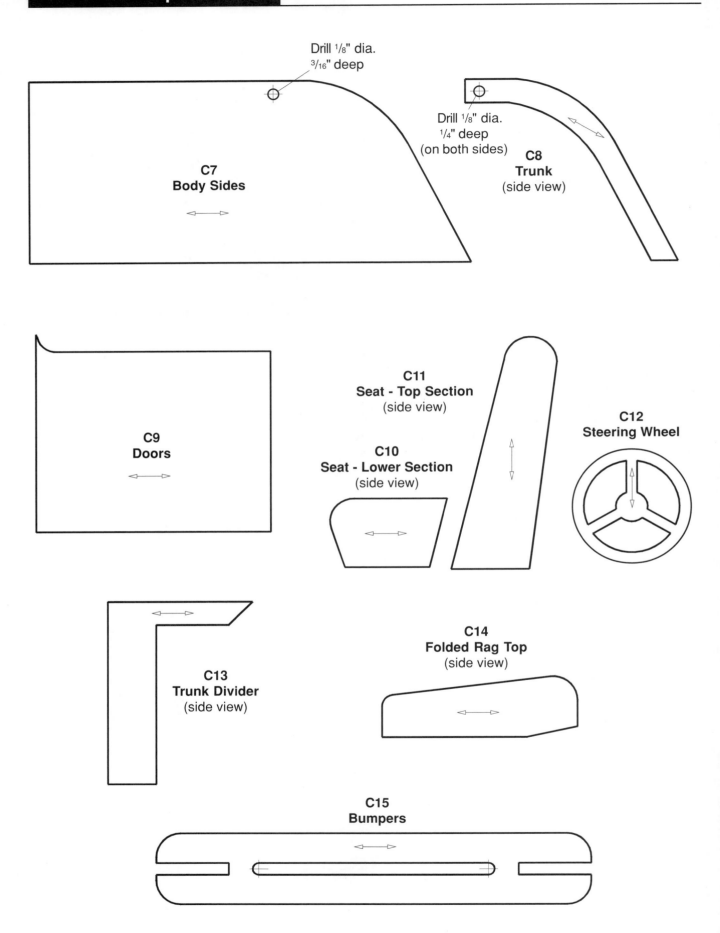

Drill ⅛" dia.
3/16" deep

**C7
Body Sides**

Drill ⅛" dia.
¼" deep
(on both sides)

**C8
Trunk**
(side view)

**C9
Doors**

**C11
Seat - Top Section**
(side view)

**C12
Steering Wheel**

**C10
Seat - Lower Section**
(side view)

**C13
Trunk Divider**
(side view)

**C14
Folded Rag Top**
(side view)

**C15
Bumpers**

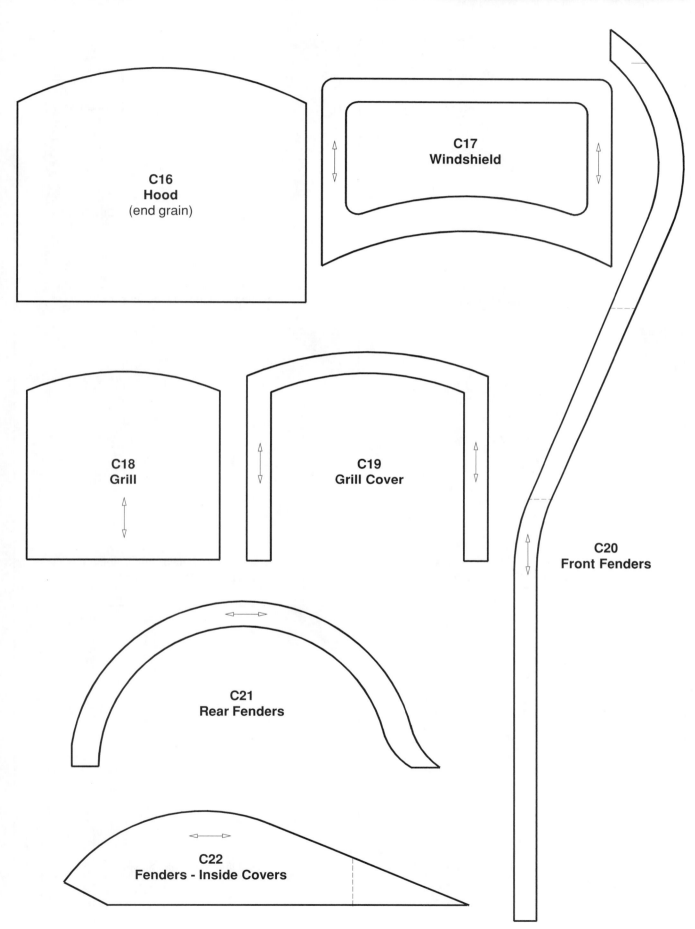

C16
Hood
(end grain)

C17
Windshield

C18
Grill

C19
Grill Cover

C20
Front Fenders

C21
Rear Fenders

C22
Fenders - Inside Covers

1

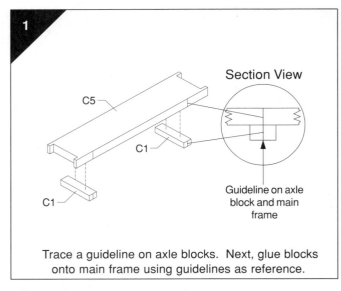

Section View

C5

C1

C1

Guideline on axle block and main frame

Trace a guideline on axle blocks. Next, glue blocks onto main frame using guidelines as reference.

2

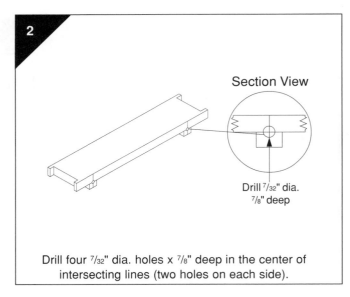

Section View

Drill $^7/_{32}$" dia. $^7/_8$" deep

Drill four $^7/_{32}$" dia. holes x $^7/_8$" deep in the center of intersecting lines (two holes on each side).

3

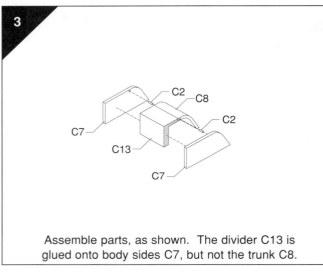

C2   C8

C7

C2

C13

C7

Assemble parts, as shown. The divider C13 is glued onto body sides C7, but not the trunk C8.

4

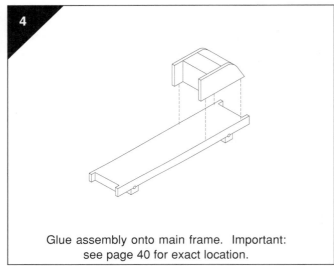

Glue assembly onto main frame. Important: see page 40 for exact location.

5

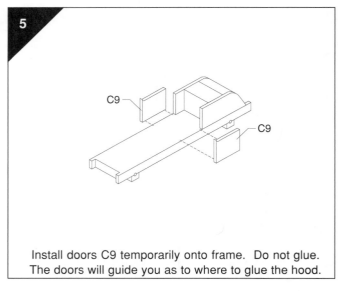

C9

C9

Install doors C9 temporarily onto frame. Do not glue. The doors will guide you as to where to glue the hood.

6

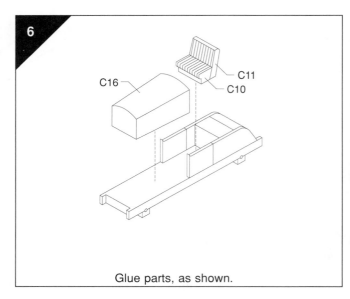

C11

C16

C10

Glue parts, as shown.

7

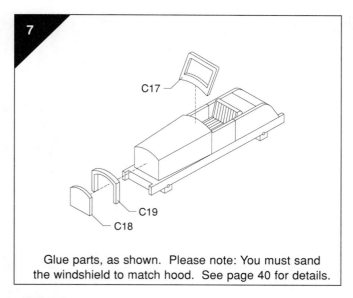

Glue parts, as shown. Please note: You must sand the windshield to match hood. See page 40 for details.

8

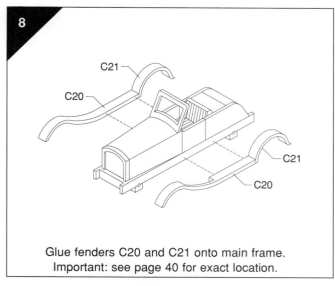

Glue fenders C20 and C21 onto main frame. Important: see page 40 for exact location.

9

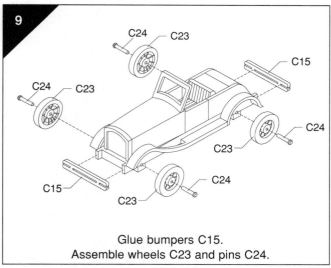

Glue bumpers C15. Assemble wheels C23 and pins C24.

10

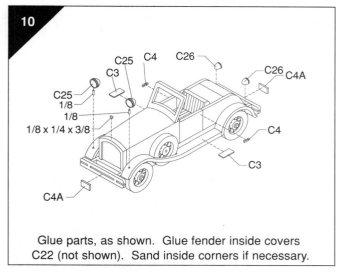

Glue parts, as shown. Glue fender inside covers C22 (not shown). Sand inside corners if necessary.

11

Cut out opening to match (contour) seat.

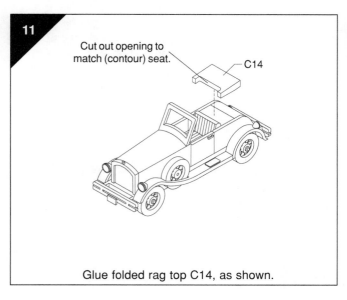

Glue folded rag top C14, as shown.

12

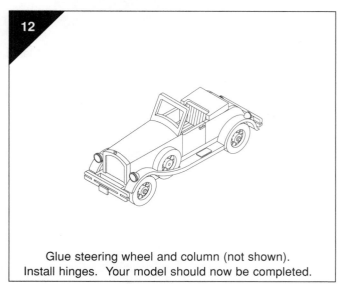

Glue steering wheel and column (not shown). Install hinges. Your model should now be completed.

The section drawing below shows where to glue body sides C7, front fenders C20 and rear fenders C21.

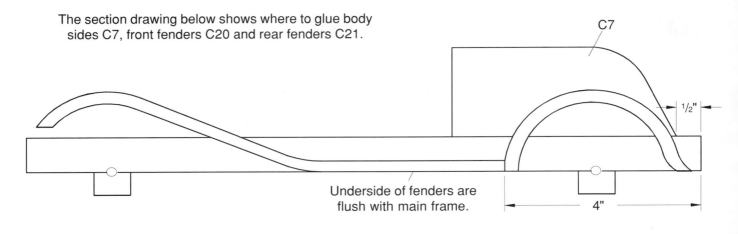

C7

1/2"

4"

Underside of fenders are flush with main frame.

Bottom must be sanded to match hood. The best tool for this task is a sanding drum mounted in your drill press.

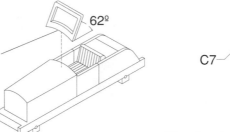

62º

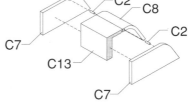

C2   C8

C7   C2

C13

C7

The drawing above shows that parts must be assembled at the same time. Glue only the trunk divider G13 onto the body sides C7.

Important steps for making the hood

Step 1:

Trace a guideline, as shown below.

Step 2:

Adjust (tilt) the table on your surface sander so that it removes 1/4" off the lower section but doesn't remove material on the top surface (it should follow your guideline).

Step 3:

Lay the material upright. Sand off material until you reach the pattern.

Step 4:

Lay the material on its flat surface, then trace two guidelines that will ensure that you remove 1/4" off on each side of the front section on your hood. Important: the table on your machine should not be tilted when sanding these surfaces.

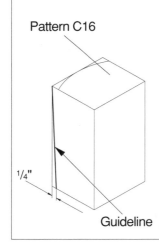

Pattern C16

1/4"

Guideline

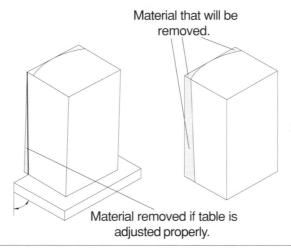

Material removed if table is adjusted properly.

Material that will be removed.

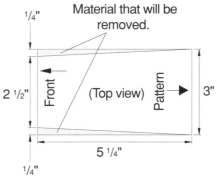

Material that will be removed.

1/4"

2 1/2"   Front   (Top view)   Pattern   3"

1/4"

5 1/4"

Late-1920s Delivery Truck

Step 1

Start by cutting materials needed using the List of Materials on pages 43 and 44. **Pay attention to the rough and finished size, and identify parts as they are cut.**

Step 2

Parts D1 to D8 are already complete. Parts D9 to D14 will need a few more steps. See the Parts Drawing section on pages 45 and 46 for more details.

Step 3

Parts D15 to D25 require removing the Full-Sized Patterns sheet found on pages 107 and 109 of the Appendix. Cut out the patterns, leaving approximately $1/16$" all around, and place on the proper piece of wood. Patterns can be secured to the wood using either spray adhesive or rubber cement. If using the latter, cut and sand the part first to finished size. If drilling is required, mark the hole by inserting an awl or nail through the pattern into the wood. Remove the pattern before drilling. (Note: arrows found on patterns indicate grain direction.)

You should have no trouble determining which surface to attach most of the patterns. Some parts, however, can be confusing since the pattern could fit on more than one surface. The drawings in Figure 1 indicate exactly which surface to attach the patterns for these parts.

Step 4

Follow the Assembly Drawings on pages 49, 50 and 51 to complete your model.

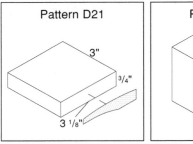
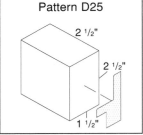

Fig. 1

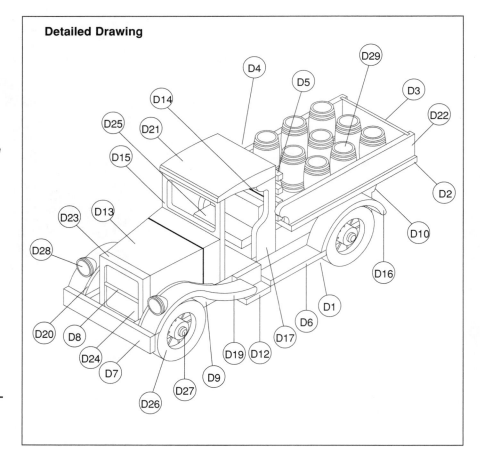

Detailed Drawing

Late-1920s Delivery Truck

Part	Description	Qty.	T	W	L	Material	*
D1	Axle Blocks	2	1/2"	3/4"	3"	Maple	F
D2	Box Floor	1	1/4"	4"	6 1/2"	Mahogony	F
D3	Box Gate	1	1/8"	1"	3 1/2"	Pine	F
D4	Vertical Braces	2	1/4"	1/2"	2 1/2"	Pine	F
D5	Horizontal Braces	4	1/4"	1/4"	3"	Pine	F
D6	Runners	2	1/4"	3/4"	2 7/8"	Mahogony	F
D7	Front Bumper	1	1/4"	3/4"	4 1/2"	Oak	F
D8	Grill - Horizontal Trim	1	1/8" dia.		1 3/4"	Maple Dowel	F
D9	Main Frame	1	3/4"	3"	12 1/8"	Maple	F
D10	Secondary Frame	1	1"	3"	6"	Mahogony	F
D11	Steering Column	1	1/4" dia.		1 1/16"	Mahogony	F
D12	Steps	2	3/4"	1"	1 1/4"	Mahogony	F
D13	Hood	1	2"	3"	3 1/4"	Mahogony	F
D14	Cabin Back	1	1/4"	2 1/2"	3 1/2"	Mahogony	F
D15	Cabin Front	1	1/4"	3 1/8"	4"	Mahogony	R
D16	Rear Fenders	2	3/4"	1 5/8"	3 5/8"	Pine	R
D17	Cabin Sides	2	1/4"	1 1/8"	3 3/4"	Mahogony	R
D18	Steering Wheel	1	1/8"	1 3/8"	1 3/8"	Maple	R
D19	Front Fenders	2	3/4"	1 3/4"	4 5/8"	Pine	R
D20	Fender - Inside Covers	2	1/8"	1 1/8"	3 1/4"	Pine	R

(continued on next page)

Part	Description	Qty.	T	W	L	Material	*
D21	Roof	1	³/₄"	3"	3 ¹/₈"	Mahogony	R
D22	Box Sides	2	¹/₄"	1 ¹/₈"	7 ¹/₈"	Mahogony	R
D23	Grill Cover	1	³/₈"	2 ¹/₂"	2 ³/₄"	Pine	R
D24	Grill	1	¹/₄"	1 ⁷/₈"	2 ¹/₈"	Oak	R
D25	Seat	1	1 ¹/₂"	2 ¹/₂"	2 ¹/₂"	Oak	R
D26	Wheels	4	2 ¹/₂" dia. x ⁷/₁₆" thick			Hard Wood	$
D27	Wheel Pins	4	¹/₄" dia. x 1 ¹/₄" long			Hard Wood	$
D28	Headlights	2	³/₄" dia. x ⁵/₈" long			Hard Wood	$
D29	Barrels	10	1 ¹/₈" dia. x 1 ⁵/₈" high			Hard Wood	$

T = Thickness	**R** = Rough size
W = Width	**F** = Finished size
L = Length	**$** = Parts to be purchased

Instructions for cutting and shaping materials

R = Rough size

The material is cut oversized so you have ample room to apply the patterns on the surface. Sanding is not required at this point.

F = Finished size

Carefully cut and sand materials to specified dimensions, making sure surfaces are square and parallel.

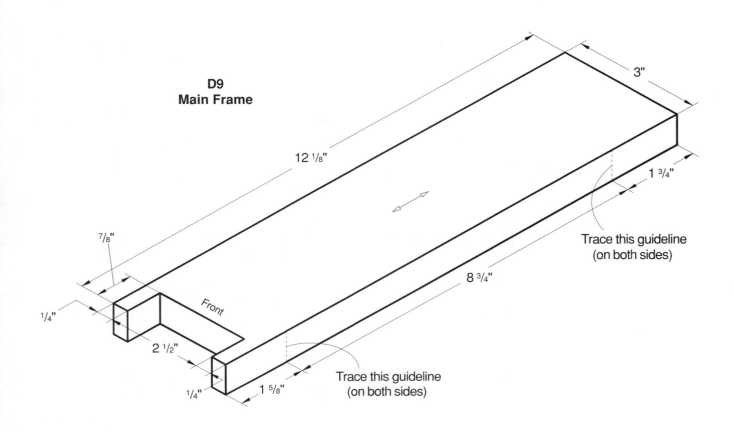

D9
Main Frame

3"

12 ⅛"

1 ¾"

Trace this guideline
(on both sides)

⅞"

8 ¾"

Front

¼"

2 ½"

¼"

1 ⅝"

Trace this guideline
(on both sides)

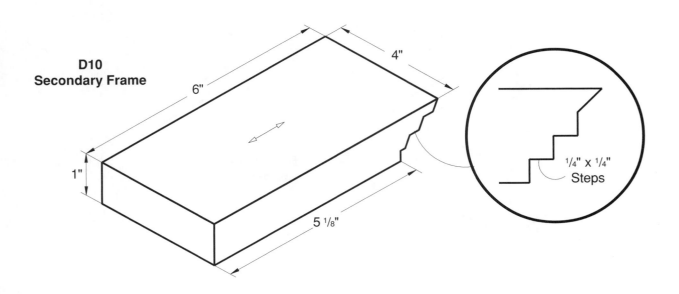

D10
Secondary Frame

4"

6"

1"

5 ⅛"

¼" x ¼"
Steps

D11
Steering Column

7/8"

1/4" dia. dowel

1 1/16"

D12
Steps

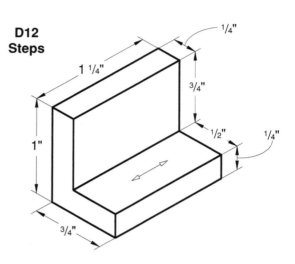

1 1/4"

1/4"

3/4"

1/2"

1/4"

1"

3/4"

D13
Hood

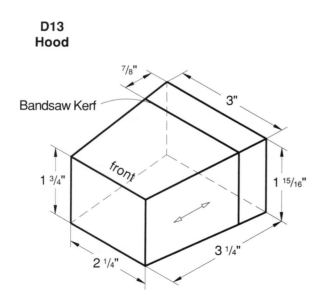

7/8"

Bandsaw Kerf

3"

front

1 3/4"

1 15/16"

2 1/4"

3 1/4"

D14
Cabin Back

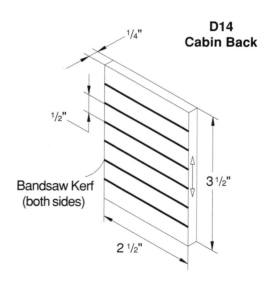

1/4"

1/2"

Bandsaw Kerf
(both sides)

3 1/2"

2 1/2"

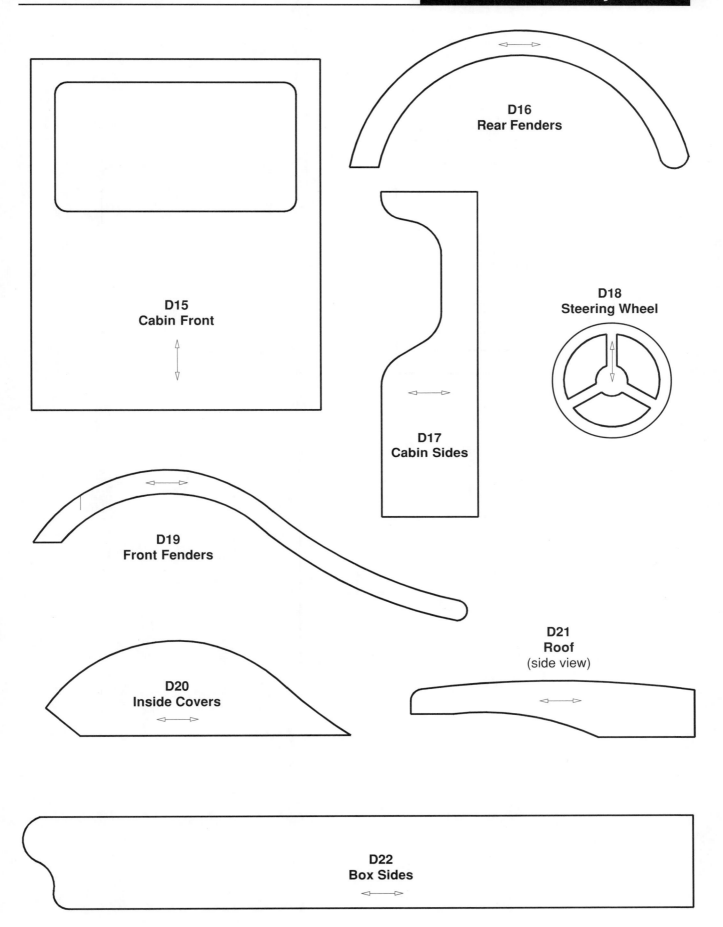

D16
Rear Fenders

D15
Cabin Front

D18
Steering Wheel

D17
Cabin Sides

D19
Front Fenders

D21
Roof
(side view)

D20
Inside Covers

D22
Box Sides

D23
Grill Cover

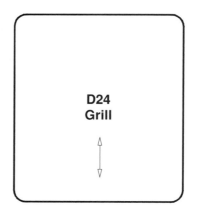

D24
Grill

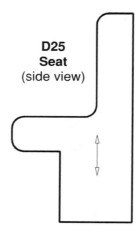

D25
Seat
(side view)

1

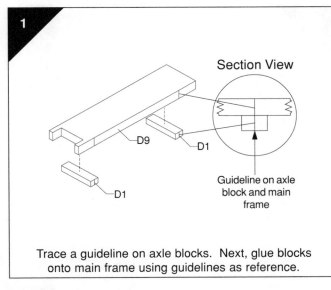

Section View

D9

D1

D1

Guideline on axle block and main frame

Trace a guideline on axle blocks. Next, glue blocks onto main frame using guidelines as reference.

2

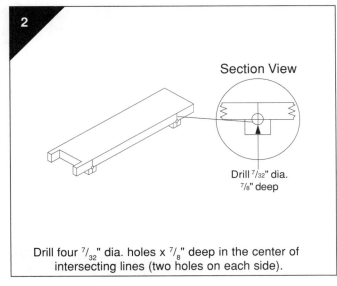

Section View

Drill $^7/_{32}$" dia. $^7/_8$" deep

Drill four $^7/_{32}$" dia. holes x $^7/_8$" deep in the center of intersecting lines (two holes on each side).

3

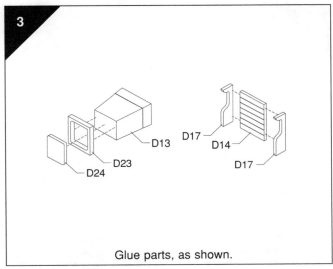

D13

D17

D14

D23

D24

D17

Glue parts, as shown.

4

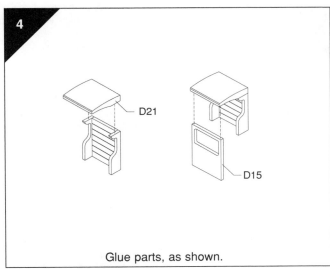

D21

D15

Glue parts, as shown.

5

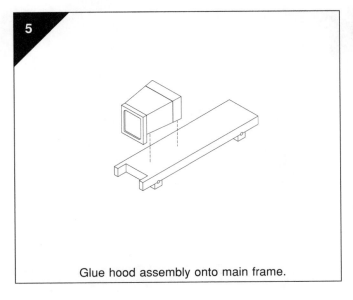

Glue hood assembly onto main frame.

6

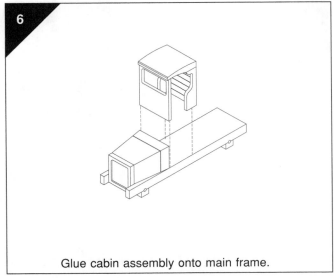

Glue cabin assembly onto main frame.

7

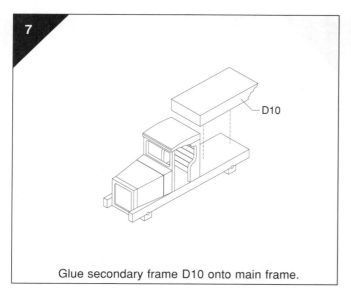

Glue secondary frame D10 onto main frame.

8

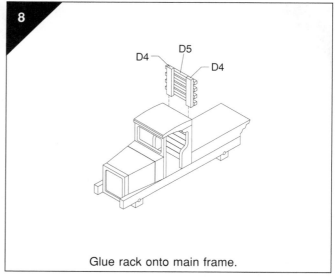

Glue rack onto main frame.

9

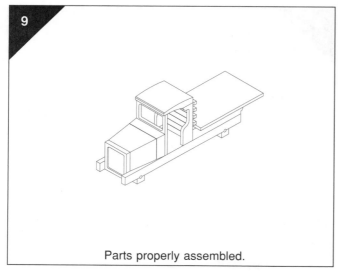

Parts properly assembled.

10

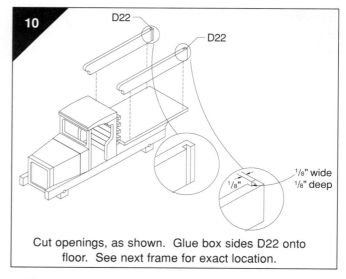

Cut openings, as shown. Glue box sides D22 onto floor. See next frame for exact location.

11

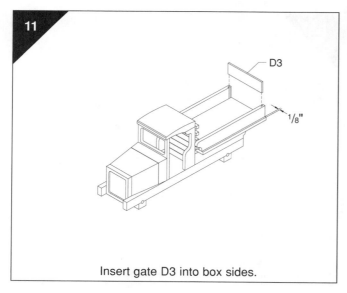

Insert gate D3 into box sides.

12

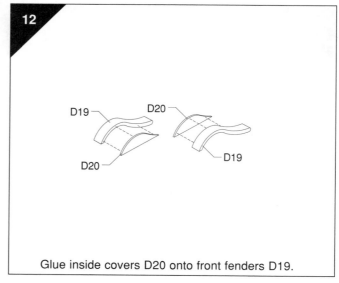

Glue inside covers D20 onto front fenders D19.

13

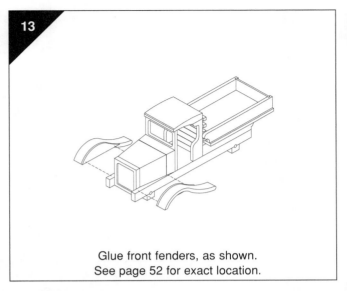

Glue front fenders, as shown.
See page 52 for exact location.

14

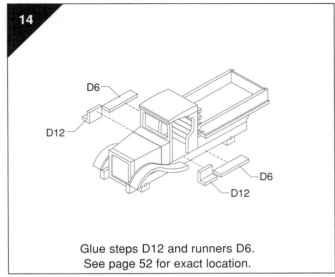

Glue steps D12 and runners D6.
See page 52 for exact location.

15

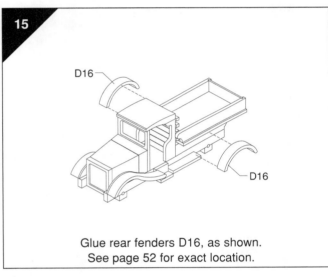

Glue rear fenders D16, as shown.
See page 52 for exact location.

16

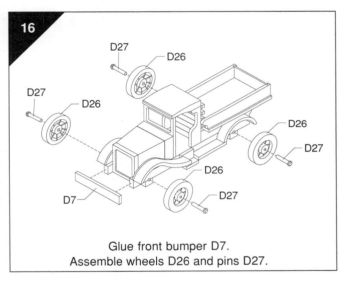

Glue front bumper D7.
Assemble wheels D26 and pins D27.

17

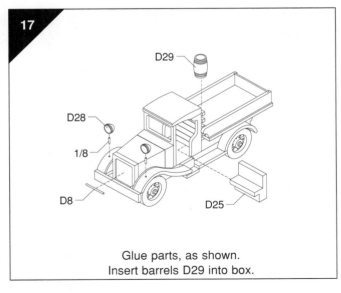

Glue parts, as shown.
Insert barrels D29 into box.

18

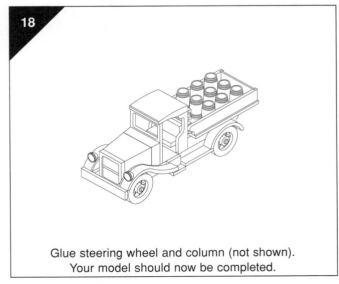

Glue steering wheel and column (not shown).
Your model should now be completed.

The section drawing below shows where to glue cabin sides D17, runners D6, steps D12, rear fenders D16 and front fenders D19.

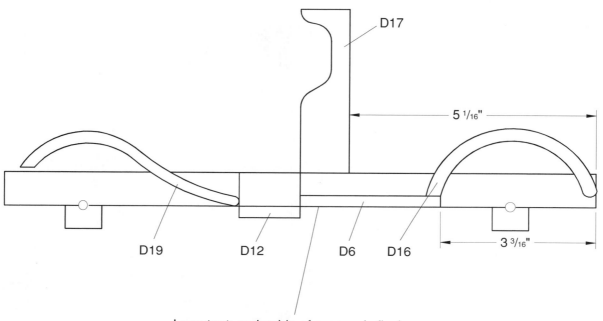

Important: underside of runners is flush with underside of main frame.

Late-1920s Town Sedan

Step 1

Start by cutting materials needed using the List of Materials on pages 55 and 56. **Pay attention to the rough and finished size, and identify parts as they are cut.**

Step 2

Parts E1 to E4 are already complete. Parts E5 to E7 will need a few more steps. See the Parts Drawing section on page 57 for more details.

Step 3

Parts E8 to E24 require removing the Full-Sized Patterns sheet found on pages 109, 111 and 113 of the Appendix. Cut out the patterns, leaving approximately $^1/_{16}$" all around, and place on the proper piece of wood. Patterns can be secured to the wood using either spray adhesive or rubber cement. If using the latter, cut and sand the part first to finished size. If drilling is required, mark the hole by inserting an awl or nail through the pattern into the wood. Remove the pattern before drilling. (Note: arrows found on patterns indicate grain direction.)

You should have no trouble determining which surface to attach most of the patterns. Some parts, however, can be confusing since the pattern could fit on more than one surface. The drawings in Figure 1 indicate exactly which surface to attach the patterns for these parts.

Step 4

Follow the Assembly Drawings on pages 60 and 61 to complete your model.

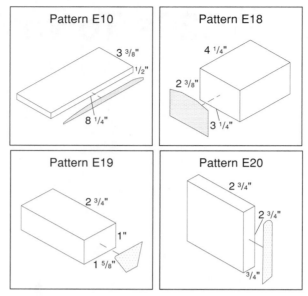

Fig. 1

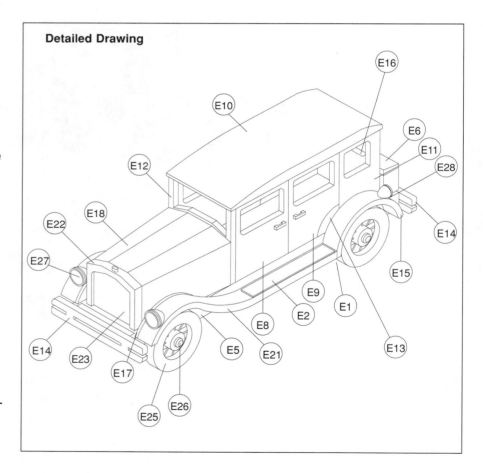

Detailed Drawing

Part	Description	Qty.	T	W	L	Material	*
E1	Axle Blocks	2	1/2"	3/4"	3 1/4"	Maple	F
E2	Floor Boards	2	1/16"	5/8"	4 1/4"	Mahogony	F
E3	Radiator Cap	1	1/8"	1/4"	3/8"	Mahogony	F
E4	Door Handles	4	1/8"	1/8"	1/2"	Maple	F
E5	Main Frame	1	3/4"	3 1/4"	13 3/4"	Maple	F
E6	Trunk	1	1 1/8"	1 7/8"	3"	Oak	F
E7	Steering Column	1	1/4" dia.		1 13/16"	Maple Dowel	F
E8	Front Doors	2	1/4"	3 3/4"	2 3/4"	Mahogony	R
E9	Rear Doors	2	1/4"	3 3/4"	2 3/4"	Mahogony	R
E10	Roof	1	1/2"	3 3/8"	8 1/4"	Mahogony	F
E11	Cabin Sides - Rear Section	2	1/4"	3 3/4"	2 3/8"	Mahogony	R
E12	Cabin Front	1	1/4"	3 1/2"	3 3/4"	Mahogony	R
E13	Cabin Side Covers	2	1/4"	1 1/4"	1 1/4"	Mahogony	R
E14	Bumpers	2	1/4"	1"	5"	Oak	R
E15	Rear Fenders	2	3/4"	1 7/8"	3 3/4"	Pine	R
E16	Cabin Back	1	1/4"	3"	3 3/4"	Mahogony	R
E17	Fender - Inside Covers	2	1/8"	1 1/8"	3 1/2"	Pine	R
E18	Hood	1	2 3/8"	3 1/4"	4 1/4"	Mahogony	F
E19	Seats - Lower Sections	2	1"	2 3/4"	1 5/8"	Pine	R
E20	Seats - Top Sections	2	3/4"	2 3/4"	2 3/4"	Pine	R

(continued on next page)

Part	Description	Qty.	T	W	L	Material	*
E21	Front Fenders	2	3/4"	1 7/8"	9 5/8"	Pine	R
E22	Grill Cover	1	3/8"	2 3/4"	2 1/2"	Pine	R
E23	Grill	1	1/4"	2 1/4"	2 1/4"	Oak	R
E24	Steering Wheel	1	1/8"	1 3/8"	1 3/8"	Maple	R
E25	Wheels	5	2 1/2" dia. x 7/16" thick			Hard Wood	$
E26	Wheel Pins	5	1/4" dia. x 1 1/4" long			Hard Wood	$
E27	Headlights	2	3/4" dia. x 5/8" long			Hard Wood	$
E28	Brakelights	2	1/2" dia. x 1/2" long			Hard Wood	$
E29	Hinges	4	12 x 16mm (7/16" x 1/2")			Brass Plated	$
E30	Hinge Screws	16	#0 x 1/4" long			Brass	$

T = Thickness
W = Width
L = Length

R = Rough size
F = Finished size
$ = Parts to be purchased

Instructions for cutting and shaping materials

R = Rough size

The material is cut oversized so you have ample room to apply the patterns on the surface. Sanding is not required at this point.

F = Finished size

Carefully cut and sand materials to specified dimensions, making sure surfaces are square and parallel.

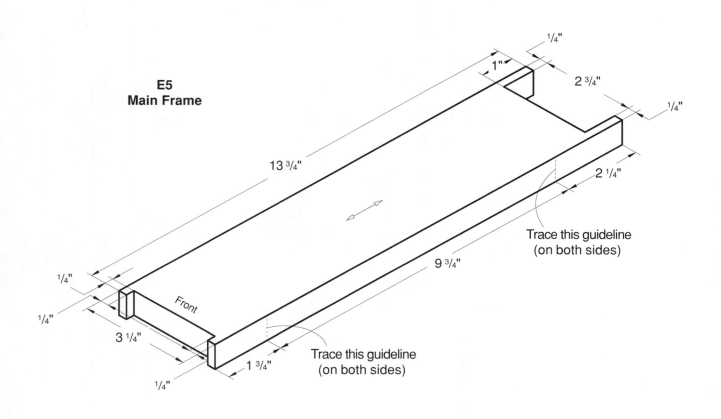

**E5
Main Frame**

1/4"

1"

2 3/4"

1/4"

13 3/4"

2 1/4"

1/4"

Trace this guideline
(on both sides)

9 3/4"

1/4"

1/4"

Front

3 1/4"

1 3/4"

1/4"

Trace this guideline
(on both sides)

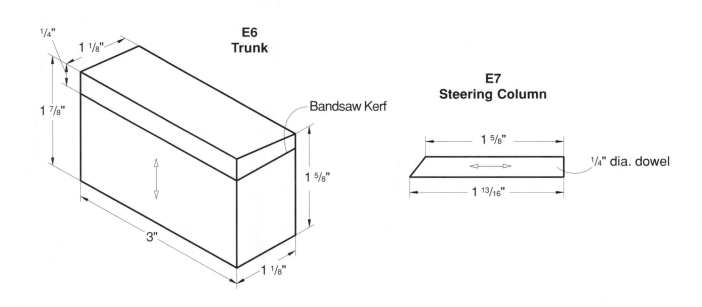

**E6
Trunk**

1/4"

1 1/8"

1 7/8"

1 5/8"

3"

1 1/8"

Bandsaw Kerf

**E7
Steering Column**

1 5/8"

1/4" dia. dowel

1 13/16"

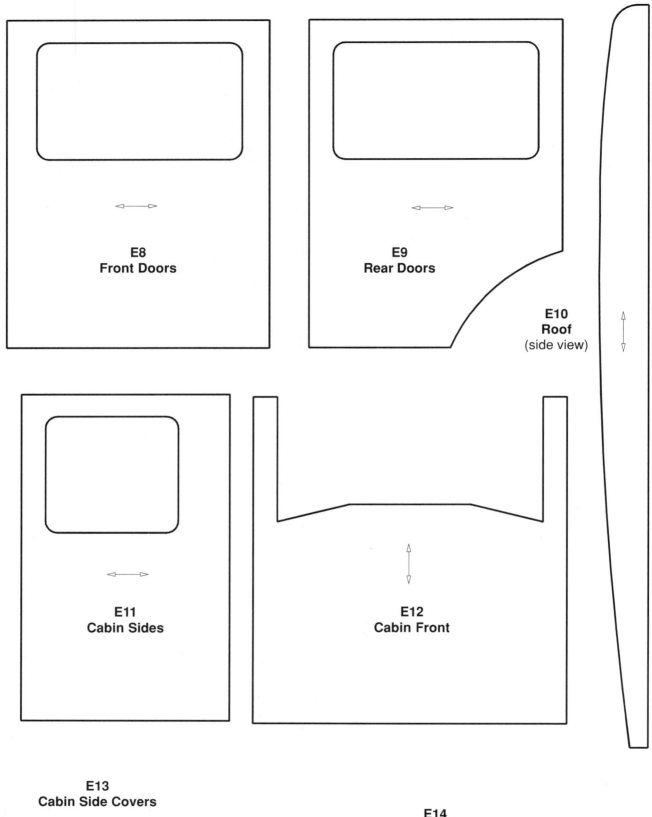

**E8
Front Doors**

**E9
Rear Doors**

**E10
Roof
(side view)**

**E11
Cabin Sides**

**E12
Cabin Front**

**E13
Cabin Side Covers**

**E14
Bumpers**

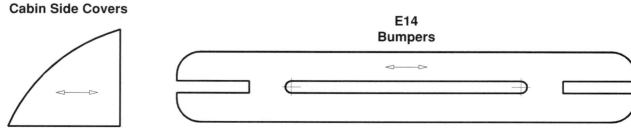

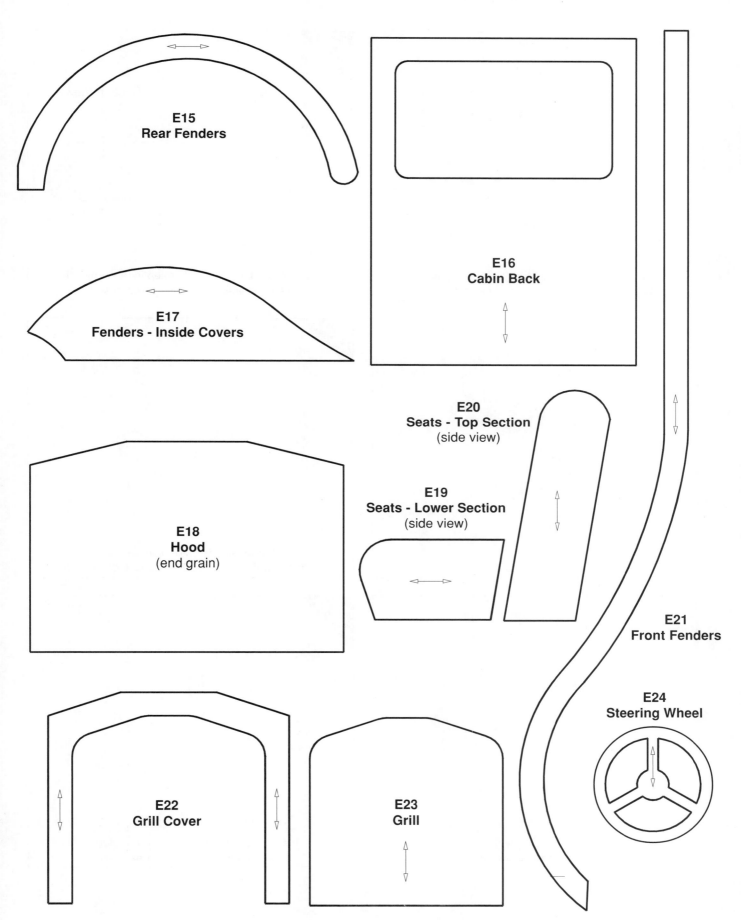

E15
Rear Fenders

E16
Cabin Back

E17
Fenders - Inside Covers

E20
Seats - Top Section
(side view)

E19
Seats - Lower Section
(side view)

E18
Hood
(end grain)

E21
Front Fenders

E24
Steering Wheel

E22
Grill Cover

E23
Grill

1

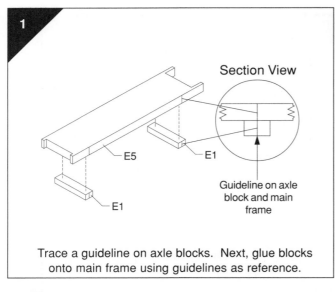

Section View

E5

E1

E1

Guideline on axle
block and main
frame

Trace a guideline on axle blocks. Next, glue blocks
onto main frame using guidelines as reference.

2

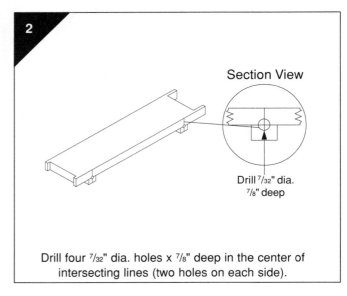

Section View

Drill $7/32$" dia.
$7/8$" deep

Drill four $7/32$" dia. holes x $7/8$" deep in the center of
intersecting lines (two holes on each side).

3

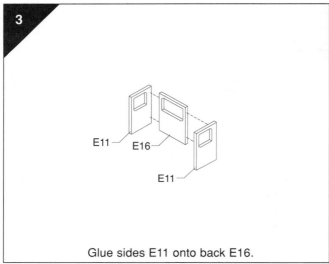

E11

E16

E11

Glue sides E11 onto back E16.

4

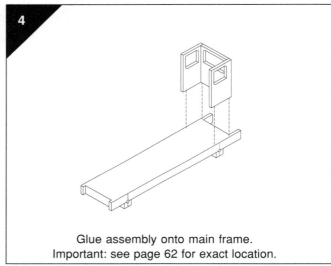

Glue assembly onto main frame.
Important: see page 62 for exact location.

5

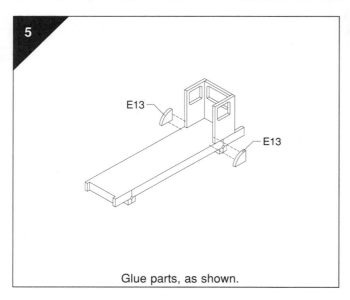

E13

E13

Glue parts, as shown.

6

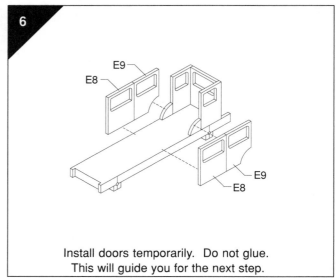

E9

E8

E9

E8

Install doors temporarily. Do not glue.
This will guide you for the next step.

7

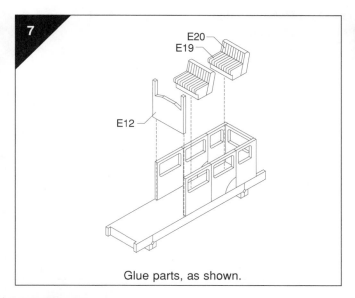

Glue parts, as shown.

8

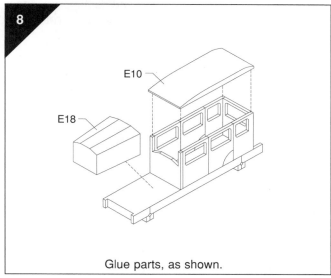

Glue parts, as shown.

9

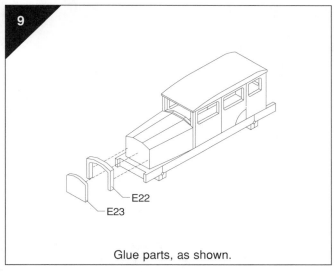

Glue parts, as shown.

10

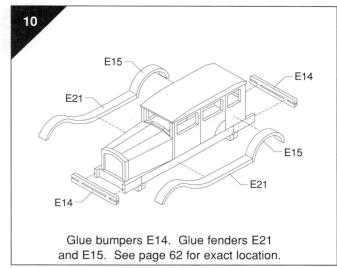

Glue bumpers E14. Glue fenders E21 and E15. See page 62 for exact location.

11

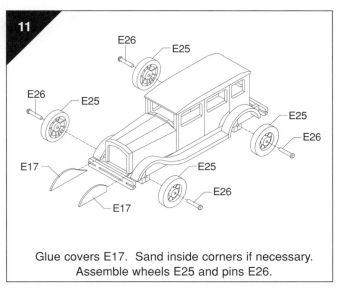

Glue covers E17. Sand inside corners if necessary. Assemble wheels E25 and pins E26.

12

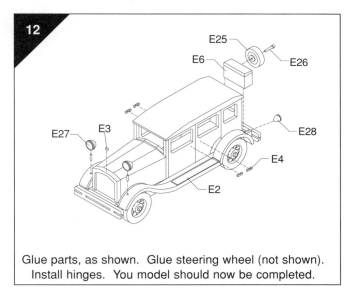

Glue parts, as shown. Glue steering wheel (not shown). Install hinges. You model should now be completed.

The section drawing below shows where to glue
cabin sides E11, rear fenders E15 and front fenders E21.

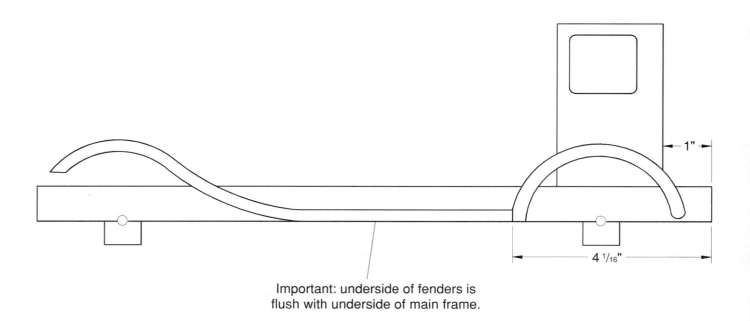

1"

4 1/16"

Important: underside of fenders is
flush with underside of main frame.

Important steps for making the hood

Step 1:

On your surface sander,
sand material as shown
below.

Step 2:

Lay the material on its
flat surface, then trace
two guidelines that will
ensure that you remove
1/4" off on each side of
the front section on your
hood.

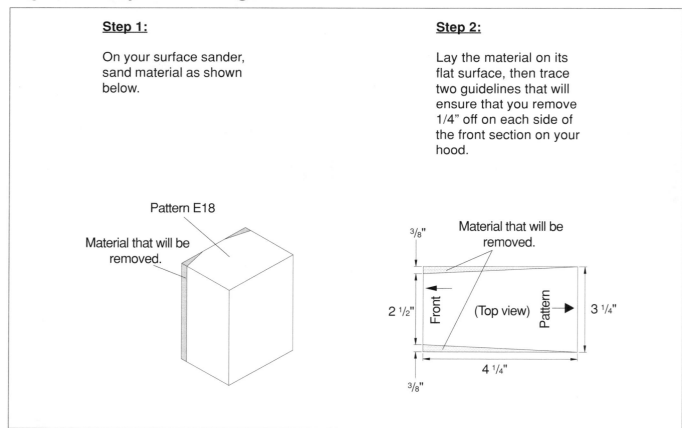

Pattern E18

Material that will be
removed.

Material that will be
removed.

3/8"

2 1/2"

Front

(Top view)

Pattern

3 1/4"

4 1/4"

3/8"

Early-1930s Coupe

Step 1

Start by cutting materials needed using the List of Materials on pages 65 and 66. **Pay attention to the rough and finished size, and identify parts as they are cut.**

Step 2

Parts F1 to F6 are already complete. Parts F7 to F10 will need a few more steps. See the Parts Drawing section on page 67 for more details.

Step 3

Parts F11 to F29 require removing the Full-Sized Patterns sheet found on pages 115 and 117 of the Appendix. Cut out the patterns, leaving approximately $1/16$" all around, and place on the proper piece of wood. Patterns can be secured to the wood using either spray adhesive or rubber cement. If using the latter, cut and sand the part first to finished size. If drilling is required, mark the hole by inserting an awl or nail through the pattern into the wood. Remove the pattern before drilling. (Note: arrows found on patterns indicate grain direction.)

You should have no trouble determining which surface to attach most of the patterns. Some parts, however, can be confusing since the pattern could fit on more than one surface. The drawings in Figure 1 indicate exactly which surface to attach the patterns for these parts. Please note: for pattern F29, you must cut out an opening for the spare wheel. Follow the instruction on page 8 to see how this step is done.

Step 4

Follow the Assembly Drawings on pages 70 and 71 to complete your model.

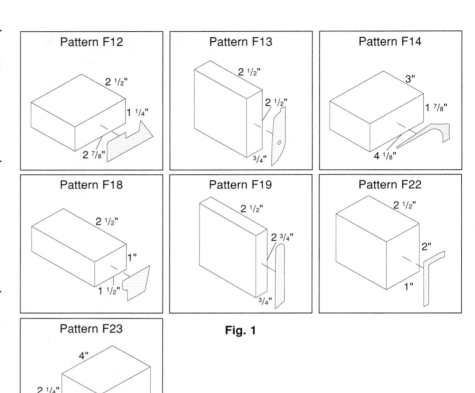

Fig. 1

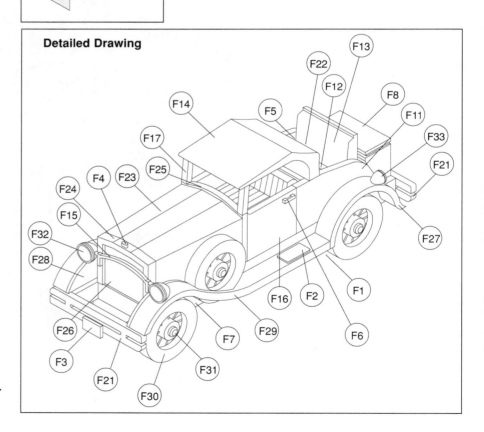

Detailed Drawing

Part	Description	Qty.	T	W	L	Material	*
F1	Axle Blocks	2	1/2"	3/4"	3"	Maple	F
F2	Floor Boards	2	1/16"	5/8"	1 1/8"	Mahogony	F
F3	Licence Plates	2	1/8"	1/2"	7/8"	Mahogony	F
F4	Radiator Cap	1	1/8"	1/4"	3/8"	Mahogony	F
F5	Rumble Seat Pivot Pins	2	1/8" dia.		3/8"	Maple Dowel	F
F6	Door Handles	2	1/8"	1/8"	1/2"	Maple	F
F7	Main Frame	1	3/4"	3"	12 7/8"	Maple	F
F8	Trunk	1	1 1/4"	2 1/2"	1 5/8"	Oak	F
F9	Steering Column	1	1/4" dia.		1"	Maple Dowel	F
F10	Rag Top Braces	2	1/8" dia.		1"	Maple Dowel	R
F11	Body Sides	2	1/4"	2 1/4"	4 1/2"	Mahogony	R
F12	Rumble Seat - Lower Section	1	1 1/4"	2 1/2"	2 7/8"	Mahogony	F
F13	Rumble Seat - Top Section	1	3/4"	2 1/2"	2 1/2"	Mahogony	F
F14	Roof	1	1 7/8"	3"	4 1/8"	Mahogony	R
F15	Headlight Frame	1	1/8"	7/8"	3 1/4"	Maple	R
F16	Doors	2	1/4"	2 3/8"	2 5/8"	Mahogony	R
F17	Cabin Braces	2	1/4"	1 1/4"	5/8"	Mahogony	R
F18	Seat - Lower Part	1	1"	2 1/2"	1 1/2"	Oak	R
F19	Seat - Top Part	1	3/4"	2 1/2"	2 3/4"	Oak	R
F20	Steering Wheel	1	1/8"	1 3/8"	1 3/8"	Maple	R

(continued on next page)

Part	Description	Qty.	T	W	L	Material	*
F21	Bumpers	2	1/4"	1"	4 3/4"	Oak	R
F22	Divider	1	1"	2 1/2"	2"	Mahogony	F
F23	Hood	1	2 1/4"	3"	4"	Mahogony	F
F24	Grill Cover	1	3/8"	2 5/8"	2 1/2"	Pine	R
F25	Cabin Front	1	1/4"	3 1/4"	2 1/2"	Mahogony	R
F26	Grill	1	1/4"	2 1/4"	2 1/4"	Oak	R
F27	Rear Fenders	2	3/4"	2"	4"	Pine	R
F28	Fender - Inside Covers	2	1/8"	1 1/8"	3 5/8"	Pine	R
F29	Front Fenders	2	3/4"	2"	9"	Pine	R
F30	Wheels	5	2 1/2" dia. x 7/16" thick			Hard Wood	$
F31	Wheel Pins	4	1/4" dia. x 1 1/4" long			Hard Wood	$
F32	Headlights	2	3/4" dia. x 5/8" long			Hard Wood	$
F33	Brakelights	2	1/2" dia. x 1/2" long			Hard Wood	$
F34	Hinges	2	12 x 16mm (7/16" x 1/2")			Brass Plated	$
F35	Hinge Screws	8	#0 x 1/4" long			Brass	$

T = Thickness	**R** = Rough size
W = Width	**F** = Finished size
L = Length	**$** = Parts to be purchased

Instructions for cutting and shaping materials

R = Rough size The material is cut oversized so you have ample room to apply the patterns on the surface. Sanding is not required at this point.

F = Finished size Carefully cut and sand materials to specified dimensions, making sure surfaces are square and parallel.

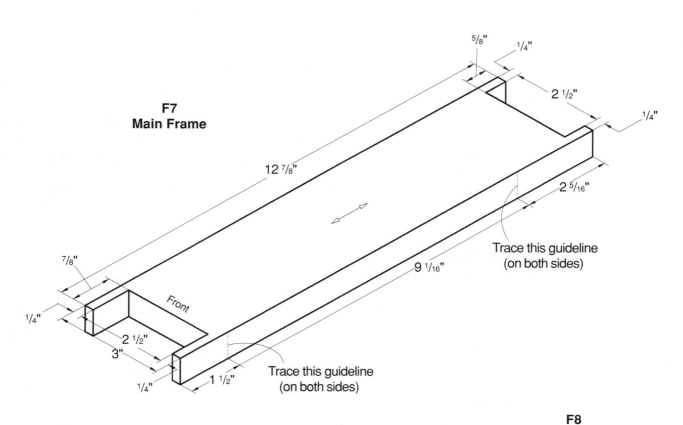

**F7
Main Frame**

12 7/8"

5/8" 1/4"

2 1/2"

1/4"

2 5/16"

Trace this guideline
(on both sides)

9 1/16"

7/8"

Front

1/4"

2 1/2"

3"

1/4"

1 1/2"

Trace this guideline
(on both sides)

**F8
Trunk**

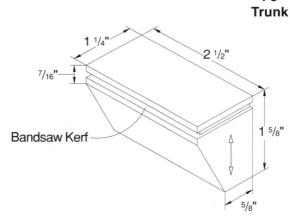

1 1/4"

2 1/2"

7/16"

1 5/8"

Bandsaw Kerf

5/8"

**F9
Steering Column**

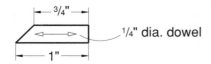

3/4"

1/4" dia. dowel

1"

**F10
Rag Top Braces**

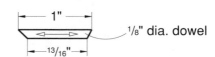

1"

1/8" dia. dowel

13/16"

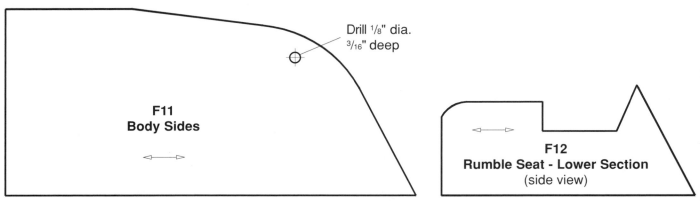

F11
Body Sides

Drill ⅛" dia.
³/₁₆" deep

F12
Rumble Seat - Lower Section
(side view)

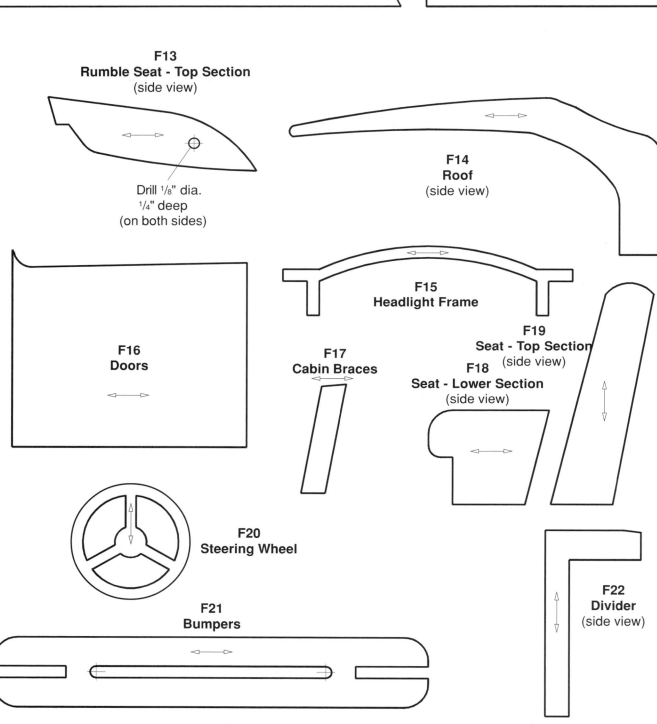

F13
Rumble Seat - Top Section
(side view)

Drill ⅛" dia.
¼" deep
(on both sides)

F14
Roof
(side view)

F15
Headlight Frame

F16
Doors

F17
Cabin Braces

F19
Seat - Top Section
(side view)

F18
Seat - Lower Section
(side view)

F20
Steering Wheel

F22
Divider
(side view)

F21
Bumpers

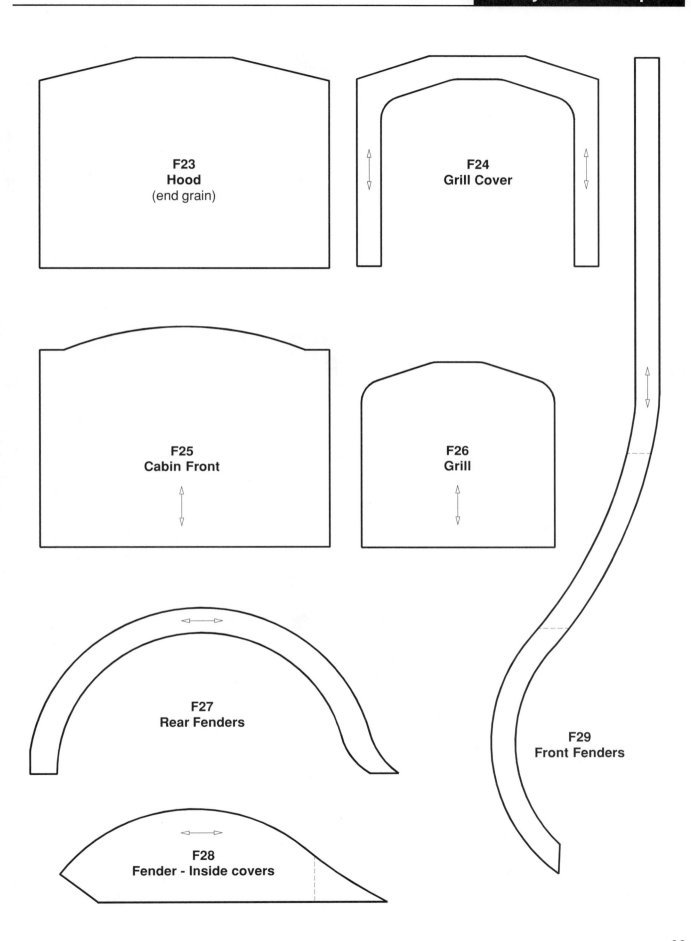

F23
Hood
(end grain)

F24
Grill Cover

F25
Cabin Front

F26
Grill

F27
Rear Fenders

F29
Front Fenders

F28
Fender - Inside covers

1

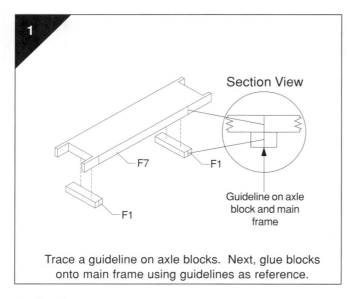

Section View

F7

F1

F1

Guideline on axle block and main frame

Trace a guideline on axle blocks. Next, glue blocks onto main frame using guidelines as reference.

2

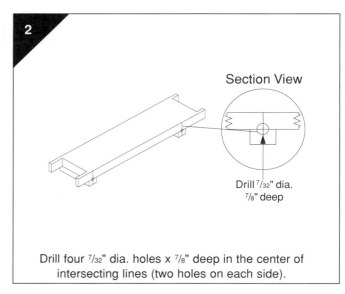

Section View

Drill $7/32$" dia. $7/8$" deep

Drill four $7/32$" dia. holes x $7/8$" deep in the center of intersecting lines (two holes on each side).

3

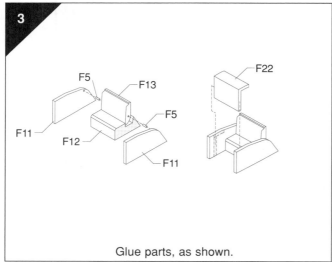

F5
F13
F22
F5
F11
F12
F11

Glue parts, as shown.

4

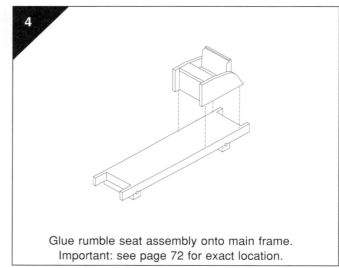

Glue rumble seat assembly onto main frame. Important: see page 72 for exact location.

5

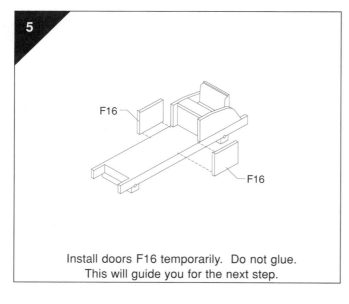

F16

F16

Install doors F16 temporarily. Do not glue. This will guide you for the next step.

6

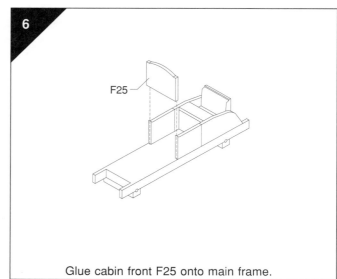

F25

Glue cabin front F25 onto main frame.

7

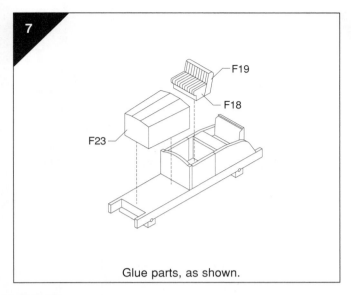

Glue parts, as shown.

8

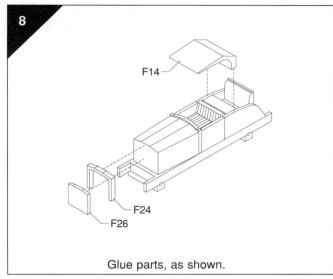

Glue parts, as shown.

9

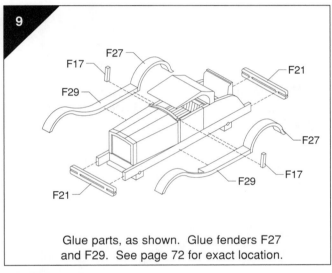

Glue parts, as shown. Glue fenders F27
and F29. See page 72 for exact location.

10

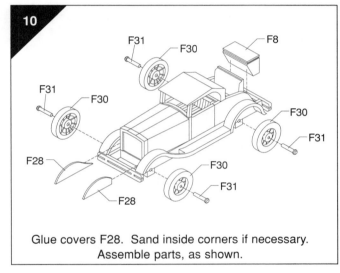

Glue covers F28. Sand inside corners if necessary.
Assemble parts, as shown.

11

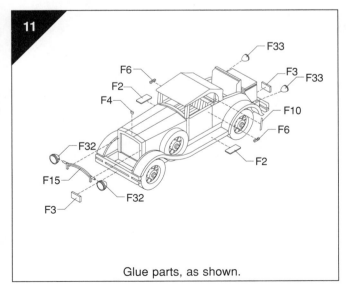

Glue parts, as shown.

12

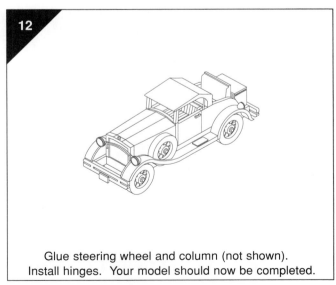

Glue steering wheel and column (not shown).
Install hinges. Your model should now be completed.

The section drawing below shows where to glue body sides F11, rear fenders F27 and front fenders F29.

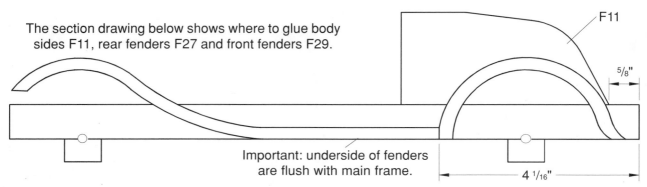

Important: underside of fenders are flush with main frame.

The drawing below shows that parts must be assembled at the same time. Glue only the rumble seat - lower section F12 onto the body sides.

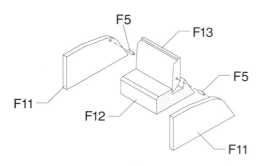

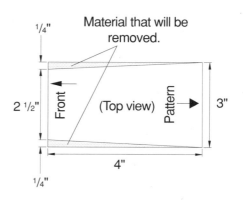

Rear view — Drill 5/8" dia.

The drawing above shows where to make the opening (window) in the back of the roof.

Important steps for making the hood

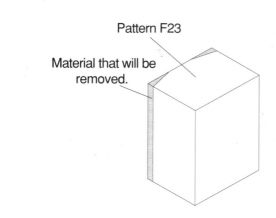

Step 1:

On your surface sander, sand material as shown below.

Step 2:

Lay the material on its flat surface, then trace two guidelines that will ensure that you remove 1/4" off on each side of the front section on your hood.

Pattern F23

Material that will be removed.

Early-1930s Sport Coupe

Step 1

Start by cutting materials needed using the List of Materials on pages 75 and 76. **Pay attention to the rough and finished size, and identify parts as they are cut.**

Step 2

Parts G1 to G6 are already complete. Parts G7 and G8 will need a few more steps. See the Parts Drawing section on page 77 for more details.

Step 3

Parts G9 to G25 require removing the Full-Sized Patterns sheet found on pages 119 and 121 of the Appendix. Cut out the patterns, leaving approximately $1/16$" all around, and place on the proper piece of wood. Patterns can be secured to the wood using either spray adhesive or rubber cement. If using the latter, cut and sand the part first to finished size. If drilling is required, mark the hole by inserting an awl or nail through the pattern into the wood. Remove the pattern before drilling. (Note: arrows found on patterns indicate grain direction.)

You should have no trouble determining which surface to attach most of the patterns. Some parts, however, can be confusing since the pattern could fit on more than one surface. The drawings in Figure 1 indicate exactly which surface to attach the patterns for these parts. Please note: for pattern G23, you must cut out an opening for the spare wheel. Follow the instruction on page 8 to see how this step is done.

Step 4

Follow the Assembly Drawings on pages 80 and 81 to complete your model.

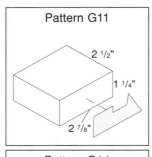

Pattern G11

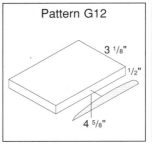

Pattern G12

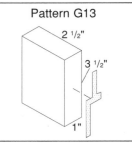

Pattern G13

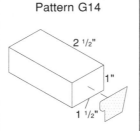

Pattern G14

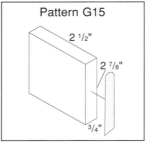

Pattern G15

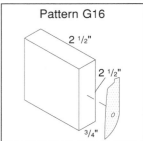

Pattern G16

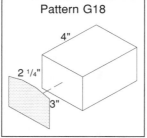

Pattern G18

Fig. 1

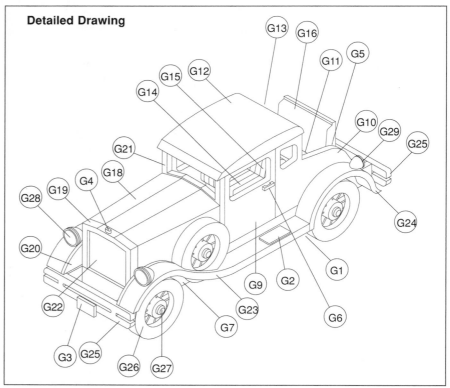

Detailed Drawing

Part	Description	Qty.	T	W	L	Material	*
G1	Axle Blocks	2	1/2"	3/4"	3"	Maple	F
G2	Floor Boards	2	1/16"	5/8"	1 1/8"	Mahogony	F
G3	Licence Plates	2	1/8"	1/2"	7/8"	Mahogony	F
G4	Radiator Cap	1	1/8"	1/4"	3/8"	Mahogony	F
G5	Rumble Seat Pivot Pins	2	1/8" dia.		3/8"	Maple Dowel	F
G6	Door Handles	2	1/8"	1/8"	1/2"	Maple	F
G7	Main Frame	1	3/4"	3"	12 3/4"	Maple	F
G8	Steering Column	1	1/4" dia.		1"	Maple Dowel	F
G9	Doors	2	1/4"	3 1/2"	2 7/8"	Mahogony	R
G10	Body Sides	2	1/4"	3 1/2"	4 1/2"	Mahogony	R
G11	Rumble Seat - Lower Section	1	1 1/4"	2 1/2"	2 7/8"	Mahogony	F
G12	Roof	1	1/2"	3 1/8"	4 5/8"	Mahogony	R
G13	Rear Window Assembly	1	1"	2 1/2"	3 1/2"	Mahogony	F
G14	Seat - Lower Part	1	1"	2 1/2"	1 1/2"	Oak	R
G15	Seat - Top Part	1	3/4"	2 1/2"	2 7/8"	Oak	R
G16	Rumble Seat - Top Section	1	3/4"	2 1/2"	2 1/2"	Mahogony	F
G17	Steering Wheel	1	1/8"	1 3/8"	1 3/8"	Maple	R
G18	Hood	1	2 1/4"	3"	4"	Mahogony	F
G19	Grill Cover	1	3/8"	2 5/8"	2 1/2"	Pine	R
G20	Fender - Inside Covers	2	1/8"	1 1/8"	3 5/8"	Pine	R

(continued on next page)

Part	Description	Qty.	T	W	L	Material	*
G21	Cabin Front	1	1/4"	3 1/4"	3 1/2"	Mahogony	R
G22	Grill	1	1/4"	2 1/4"	2 1/4"	Oak	R
G23	Front Fenders	2	3/4"	2"	9"	Pine	R
G24	Rear Fenders	2	3/4"	2"	4"	Pine	R
G25	Bumpers	2	1/4"	1"	4 3/4"	Oak	R
G26	Wheels	5	2 1/2" dia. x 7/16" thick			Hard Wood	$
G27	Wheel Pins	4	1/4" dia. x 1 1/4" long			Hard Wood	$
G28	Headlights	2	3/4" dia. x 5/8" long			Hard Wood	$
G29	Brakelights	2	1/2" dia. x 1/2" long			Hard Wood	$
G30	Hinges	2	12 x 16mm (7/16" x 1/2")			Brass Plated	$
G31	Hinge Screws	8	#0 x 1/4" long			Brass	$

T = Thickness	**R** = Rough size
W = Width	**F** = Finished size
L = Length	**$** = Parts to be purchased

Instructions for cutting and shaping materials

R = Rough size

The material is cut oversized so you have ample room to apply the patterns on the surface. Sanding is not required at this point.

F = Finished size

Carefully cut and sand materials to specified dimensions, making sure surfaces are square and parallel.

**G7
Main Frame**

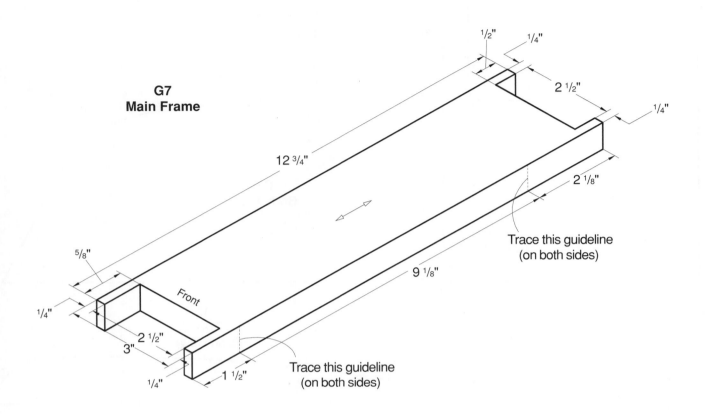

$^{1}/_{2}$" $^{1}/_{4}$"

2 $^{1}/_{2}$"

$^{1}/_{4}$"

12 $^{3}/_{4}$"

2 $^{1}/_{8}$"

Trace this guideline
(on both sides)

9 $^{1}/_{8}$"

$^{5}/_{8}$"

Front

$^{1}/_{4}$"

2 $^{1}/_{2}$"

3"

$^{1}/_{4}$"

1 $^{1}/_{2}$"

Trace this guideline
(on both sides)

**G8
Steering Column**

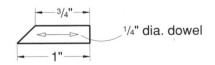

$^{3}/_{4}$"

$^{1}/_{4}$" dia. dowel

1"

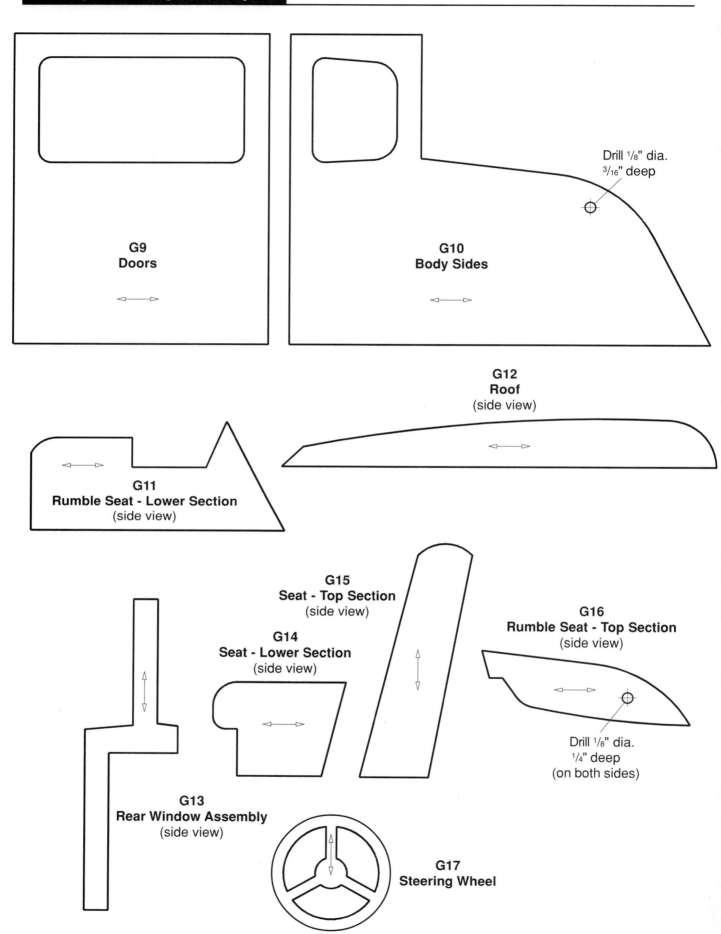

G9
Doors

G10
Body Sides

Drill 1/8" dia.
3/16" deep

G12
Roof
(side view)

G11
Rumble Seat - Lower Section
(side view)

G15
Seat - Top Section
(side view)

G14
Seat - Lower Section
(side view)

G16
Rumble Seat - Top Section
(side view)

Drill 1/8" dia.
1/4" deep
(on both sides)

G13
Rear Window Assembly
(side view)

G17
Steering Wheel

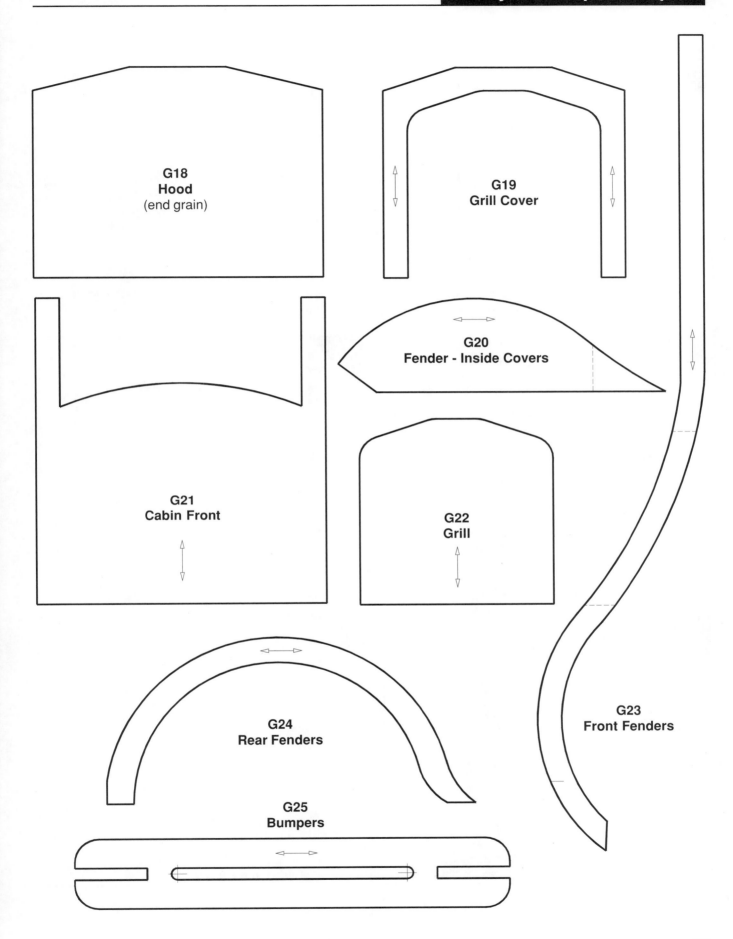

G18
Hood
(end grain)

G19
Grill Cover

G20
Fender - Inside Covers

G21
Cabin Front

G22
Grill

G23
Front Fenders

G24
Rear Fenders

G25
Bumpers

1

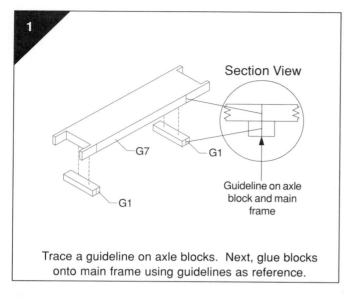

Section View

G7 — G1

G1

Guideline on axle
block and main
frame

Trace a guideline on axle blocks. Next, glue blocks
onto main frame using guidelines as reference.

2

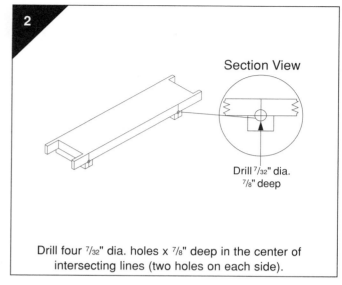

Section View

Drill ⁷/₃₂" dia.
⁷/₈" deep

Drill four ⁷/₃₂" dia. holes x ⁷/₈" deep in the center of
intersecting lines (two holes on each side).

3

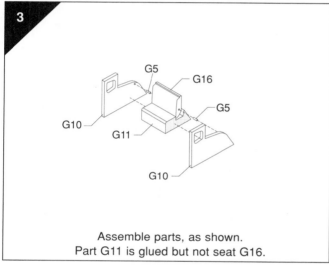

G5
G16
G5
G10
G11
G10

Assemble parts, as shown.
Part G11 is glued but not seat G16.

4

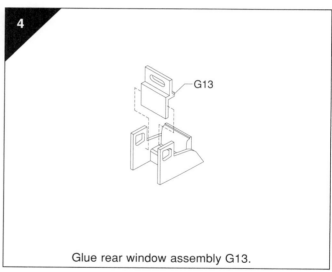

G13

Glue rear window assembly G13.

5

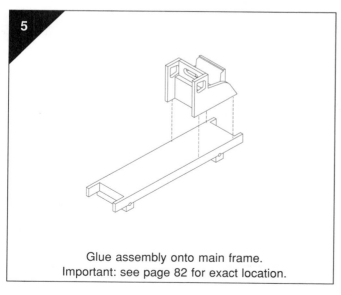

Glue assembly onto main frame.
Important: see page 82 for exact location.

6

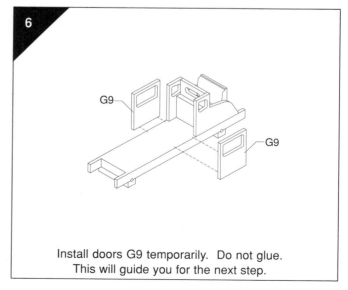

G9

G9

Install doors G9 temporarily. Do not glue.
This will guide you for the next step.

7

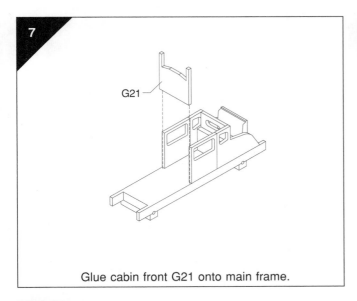

Glue cabin front G21 onto main frame.

8

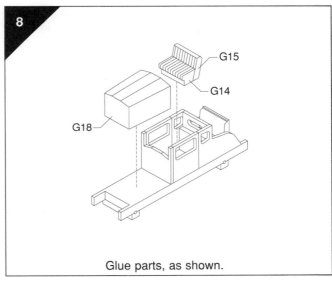

Glue parts, as shown.

9

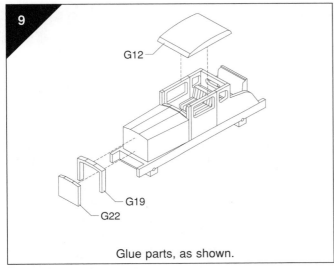

Glue parts, as shown.

10

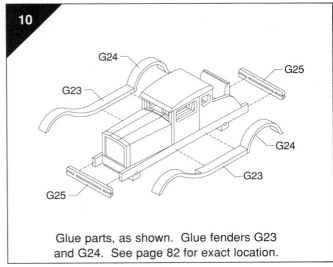

Glue parts, as shown. Glue fenders G23 and G24. See page 82 for exact location.

11

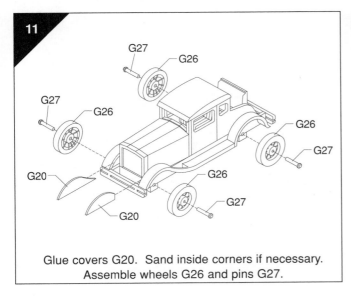

Glue covers G20. Sand inside corners if necessary. Assemble wheels G26 and pins G27.

12

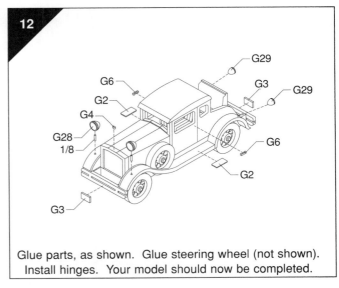

Glue parts, as shown. Glue steering wheel (not shown). Install hinges. Your model should now be completed.

The section drawing below shows where to glue body sides G10, front fenders G23 and rear fenders G24.

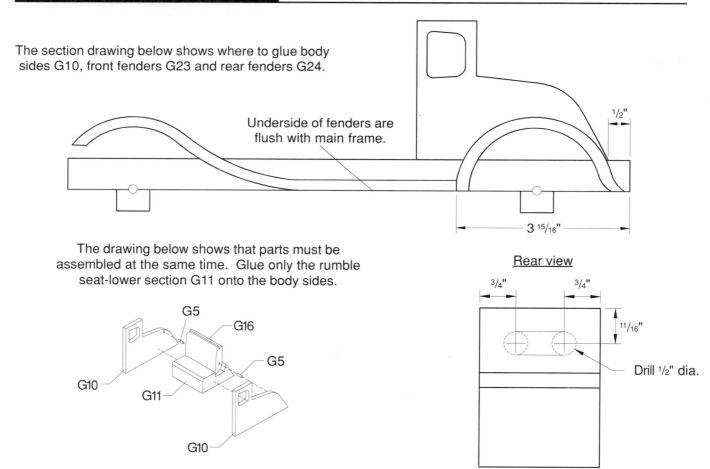

Underside of fenders are flush with main frame.

1/2"

3 15/16"

The drawing below shows that parts must be assembled at the same time. Glue only the rumble seat-lower section G11 onto the body sides.

Rear view

3/4"   3/4"

11/16"

Drill 1/2" dia.

The drawing above shows where to make the opening (window) in the back of the rear window assembly G13.

Important steps for making the hood

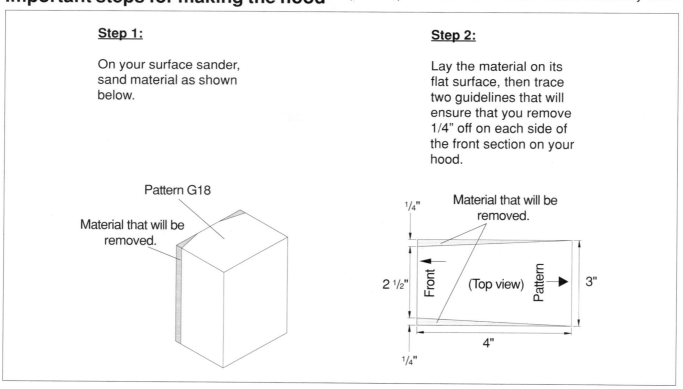

Step 1:

On your surface sander, sand material as shown below.

Pattern G18

Material that will be removed.

Step 2:

Lay the material on its flat surface, then trace two guidelines that will ensure that you remove 1/4" off on each side of the front section on your hood.

1/4"

Material that will be removed.

2 1/2"   Front   (Top view)   Pattern   3"

4"

1/4"

Mid-1930s Town Sedan

Step 1

Start by cutting materials needed using the List of Materials on pages 85 and 86. **Pay attention to the rough and finished size, and identify parts as they are cut.**

Step 2

Parts H1 to H8 are already complete. Parts H9 and H10 will need a few more steps. See the Parts Drawing section on page 87 for more details.

Step 3

Parts H11 to H26 require removing the Full-Sized Patterns sheet found on pages 123 and 125 of the Appendix. Cut out the patterns, leaving approximately 1/16" all around, and place on the proper piece of wood. Patterns can be secured to the wood using either spray adhesive or rubber cement. If using the latter, cut and sand the part first to finished size. If drilling is required, mark the hole by inserting an awl or nail through the pattern into the wood. Remove the pattern before drilling. (Note: arrows found on patterns indicate grain direction.)

You should have no trouble determining which surface to attach most of the patterns. Some parts, however, can be confusing since the pattern could fit on more than one surface. The drawings in Figure 1 indicate exactly which surface to attach the patterns for these parts. Please note: for pattern H26, you must cut out an opening for the spare wheel. Follow the instruction on page 8 to see how this step is done.

Step 4

Follow the Assembly Drawings on pages 90 and 91 to complete your model.

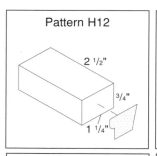
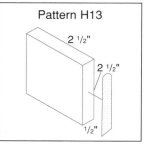
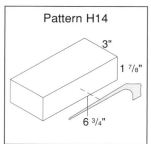
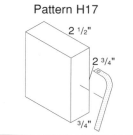
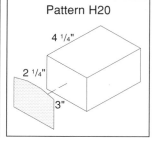

Fig. 1

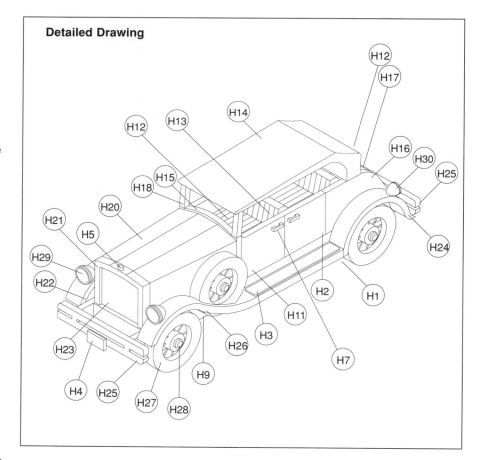

Detailed Drawing

Part	Description	Qty.	T	W	L	Material	*
H1	Axle Blocks	2	1/2"	3/4"	3"	Maple	F
H2	Rear Doors	2	1/4"	1 15/16"	2 1/8"	Mahogony	F
H3	Floor Boards	2	1/16"	5/8"	4 1/4"	Mahogony	F
H4	Licence Plates	2	1/8"	1/2"	7/8"	Mahogony	F
H5	Radiator Cap	1	1/8"	1/4"	3/8"	Mahogony	F
H6	Trunk Pivot Pins	2	1/8" dia.		3/8"	Maple Dowel	F
H7	Door Handles	4	1/8"	1/8"	1/2"	Maple	F
H8	Trunk Handle	1	1/4"	1/4"	1/2"	Maple	F
H9	Main Frame	1	3/4"	3"	13 7/8"	Maple	F
H10	Steering Column	1	1/4" dia.		7/8"	Maple Dowel	F
H11	Front Doors	2	1/4"	2 1/4"	2 3/8"	Mahogony	R
H12	Seats - Lower Sections	2	3/4"	2 1/2"	1 1/4"	Pine	R
H13	Seats - Top Sections	2	1/2"	2 1/2"	2 1/2"	Pine	R
H14	Roof	1	1 7/8"	3"	6 3/4"	Mahogony	R
H15	Cabin Front	1	1/4"	3 1/8"	2 5/8"	Mahogony	R
H16	Body Sides	2	1/4"	2 1/8"	3 3/4"	Mahogony	R
H17	Trunk	1	3/4"	2 1/2"	2 3/4"	Mahogony	F
H18	Cabin Braces	2	1/4"	1 3/8"	1/2"	Mahogony	R
H19	Steering Wheel	1	1/8"	1 3/8"	1 3/8"	Maple	R
H20	Hood	1	2 1/4"	3"	4 1/4"	Mahogony	F

(continued on next page)

Part	Description	Qty.	T	W	L	Material	*
H21	Grill Cover	1	3/8"	2 5/8"	2 1/2"	Pine	R
H22	Fender - Inside Covers	2	1/8"	1 1/8"	3 5/8"	Pine	R
H23	Grill	1	1/4"	2 1/4"	2 1/4"	Oak	R
H24	Rear Fenders	2	3/4"	2"	4"	Pine	R
H25	Bumpers	2	1/4"	1"	4 3/4"	Oak	R
H26	Front Fenders	2	3/4"	2"	10"	Pine	R
H27	Wheels	5	2 1/2" dia. x 7/16" thick			Hard Wood	$
H28	Wheel Pins	4	1/4" dia. x 1 1/4" long			Hard Wood	$
H29	Headlights	2	3/4" dia. x 5/8" long			Hard Wood	$
H30	Brakelights	2	1/2" dia. x 1/2" long			Hard Wood	$
H31	Hinges	4	12 x 16mm (7/16" x 1/2")			Brass Plated	$
H32	Hinge Screws	16	#0 x 1/4" long			Brass	$

T = Thickness
W = Width
L = Length

R = Rough size
F = Finished size
$ = Parts to be purchased

Instructions for cutting and shaping materials

R = Rough size

The material is cut oversized so you have ample room to apply the patterns on the surface. Sanding is not required at this point.

F = Finished size

Carefully cut and sand materials to specified dimensions, making sure surfaces are square and parallel.

**H9
Main Frame**

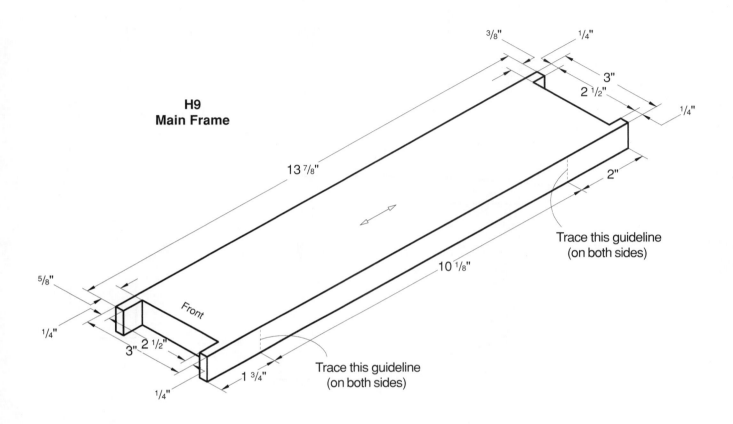

3/8"   1/4"

3"

2 1/2"

1/4"

13 7/8"

2"

Trace this guideline
(on both sides)

10 1/8"

5/8"

Front

1/4"

3"   2 1/2"

1/4"

1 3/4"

Trace this guideline
(on both sides)

**H10
Steering Column**

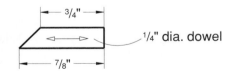

3/4"

1/4" dia. dowel

7/8"

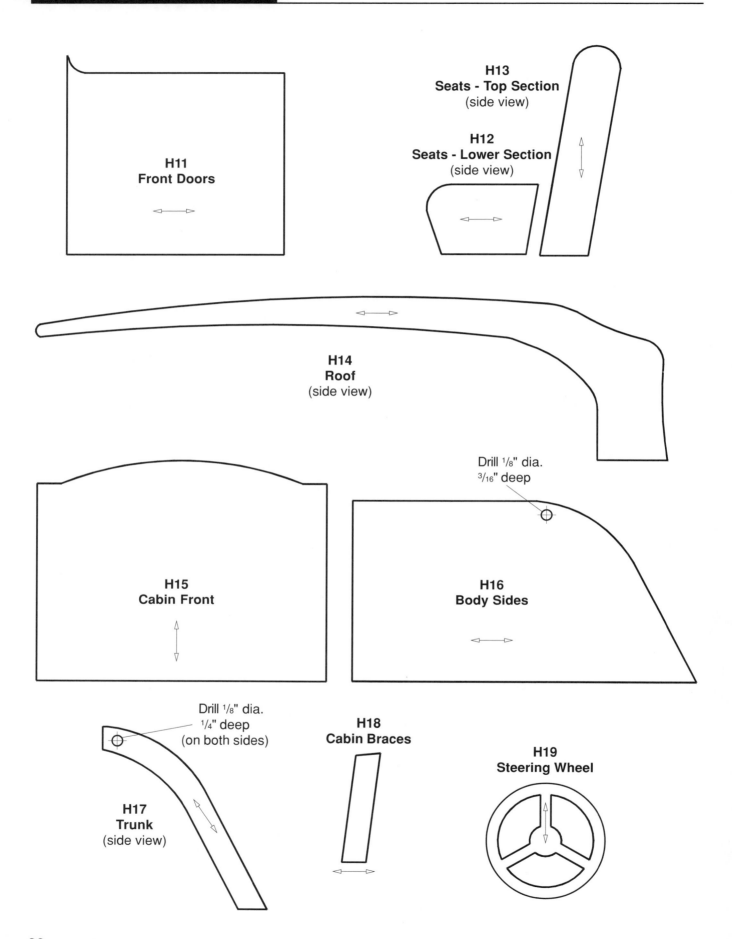

H11
Front Doors

H13
Seats - Top Section
(side view)

H12
Seats - Lower Section
(side view)

H14
Roof
(side view)

H15
Cabin Front

Drill ⅛" dia.
³⁄₁₆" deep

H16
Body Sides

Drill ⅛" dia.
¼" deep
(on both sides)

H18
Cabin Braces

H19
Steering Wheel

H17
Trunk
(side view)

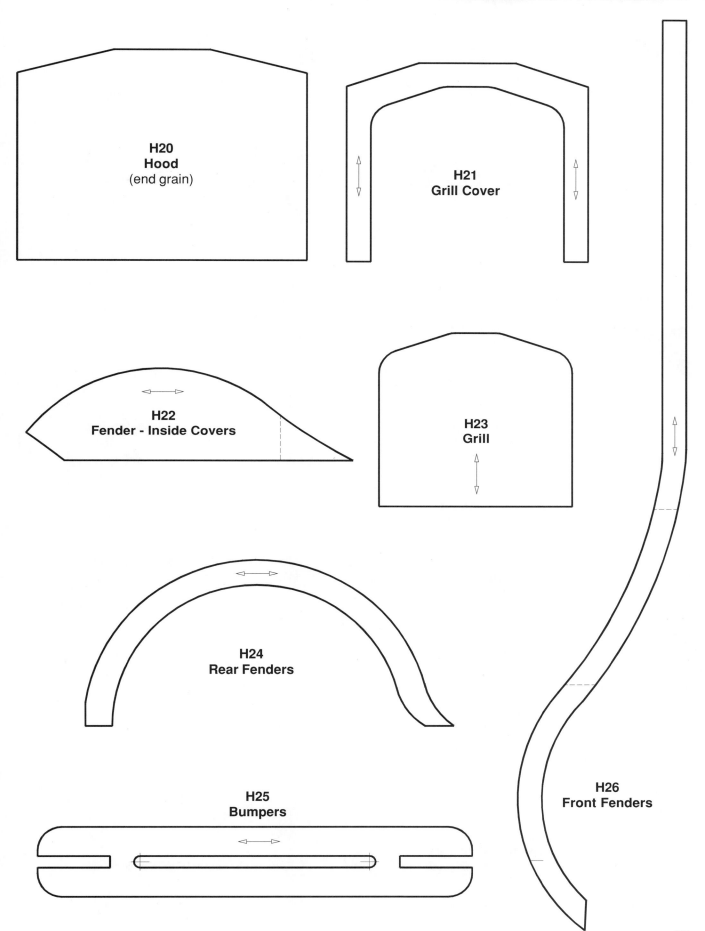

H20
Hood
(end grain)

H21
Grill Cover

H22
Fender - Inside Covers

H23
Grill

H24
Rear Fenders

H25
Bumpers

H26
Front Fenders

1

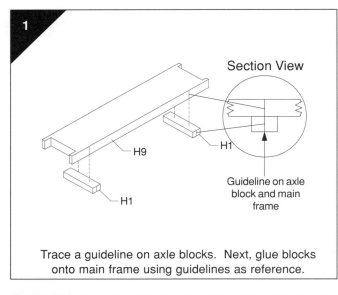

Section View

H9

H1

H1

Guideline on axle block and main frame

Trace a guideline on axle blocks. Next, glue blocks onto main frame using guidelines as reference.

2

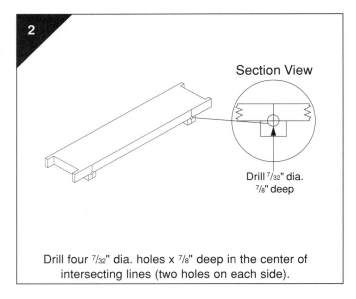

Section View

Drill $7/32$" dia. $7/8$" deep

Drill four $7/32$" dia. holes x $7/8$" deep in the center of intersecting lines (two holes on each side).

3

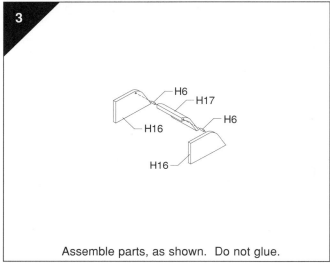

H6
H17
H6
H16
H16

Assemble parts, as shown. Do not glue.

4

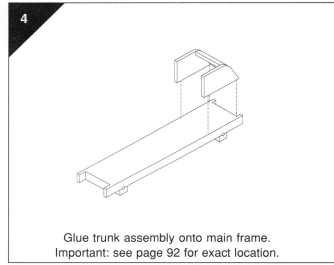

Glue trunk assembly onto main frame.
Important: see page 92 for exact location.

5

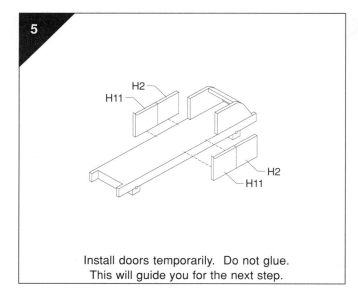

H2
H11
H2
H11

Install doors temporarily. Do not glue.
This will guide you for the next step.

6

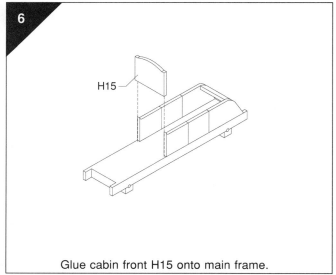

H15

Glue cabin front H15 onto main frame.

7

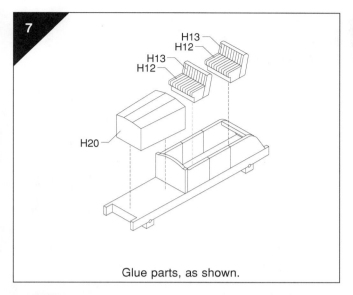

H13
H12
H13
H12
H20

Glue parts, as shown.

8

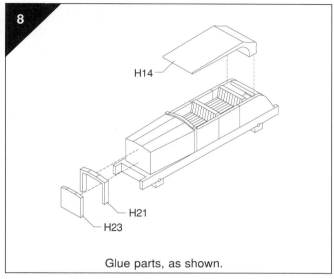

H14

H21
H23

Glue parts, as shown.

9

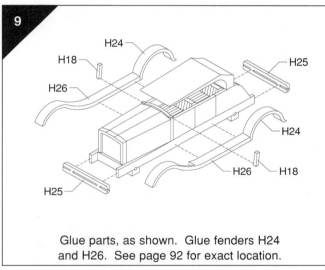

H24
H18
H26
H25
H24
H26
H18
H25

Glue parts, as shown. Glue fenders H24
and H26. See page 92 for exact location.

10

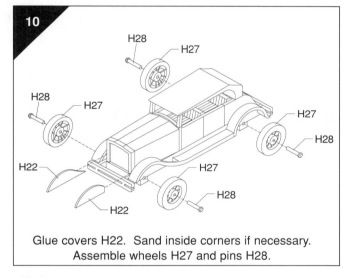

H28
H27
H28
H27
H27
H28
H22
H27
H22
H28

Glue covers H22. Sand inside corners if necessary.
Assemble wheels H27 and pins H28.

11

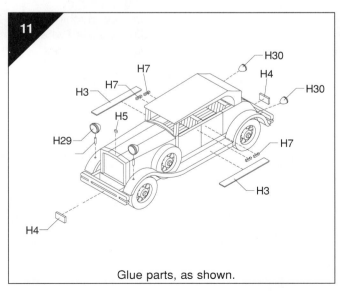

H30
H7
H4
H3
H7
H30
H5
H7
H29
H7
H3
H4

Glue parts, as shown.

12

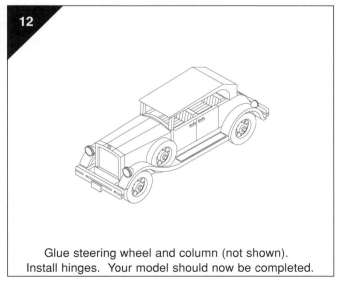

Glue steering wheel and column (not shown).
Install hinges. Your model should now be completed.

The section drawing below shows where to glue body sides H16, rear fenders H24 and front fenders H26.

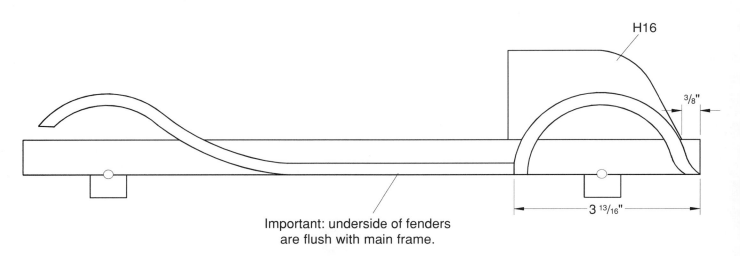

H16

3/8"

Important: underside of fenders are flush with main frame.

3 13/16"

Important steps for making the hood

Step 1:

Trace a guideline, as shown below.
Note: pattern is not exactly as shown.

Step 2:

Adjust (tilt) the table on your surface sander so that it removes 1/8" off the lower section but does not remove material on the top surface (it should follow your guideline).

Step 3:

Lay the material upright. Sand off material until you reach the pattern.

Step 4:

Lay the material on its flat surface, then trace two guidelines that will ensure that you remove 1/4" off on each side of the front section on your hood. Important: the table on your machine should not be tilted when sanding these surfaces.

Pattern H20

1/8"

Guideline

Material removed if table is adjusted properly.

Material that will be removed.

Material that will be removed.

1/4"

2 1/2"

Front

(Top view)

Pattern

3"

4 1/4"

1/4"

Appendix

Step 1 Cut out patterns, leaving approximately $1/16$" all around, and place on the proper piece of wood (which has already been identified).
Patterns can be secured to wood using either spray adhesive or rubber cement. A glue stick can also be used, but the pattern is often hard to remove afterward!

Step 2 Cut and sand the part to finished size. If drilling is required, mark the hole(s) by inserting an awl or nail through the pattern into the wood. Remove the pattern before drilling.

Step 3 Once all the parts are made for the desired model, follow the assembly drawings to complete your vehicle.

Please note: If any of the patterns become damaged before completing a part, use the originals (Full-Sized Patterns: Set One) included with each model. It can be transferred onto the wood using tracing paper.

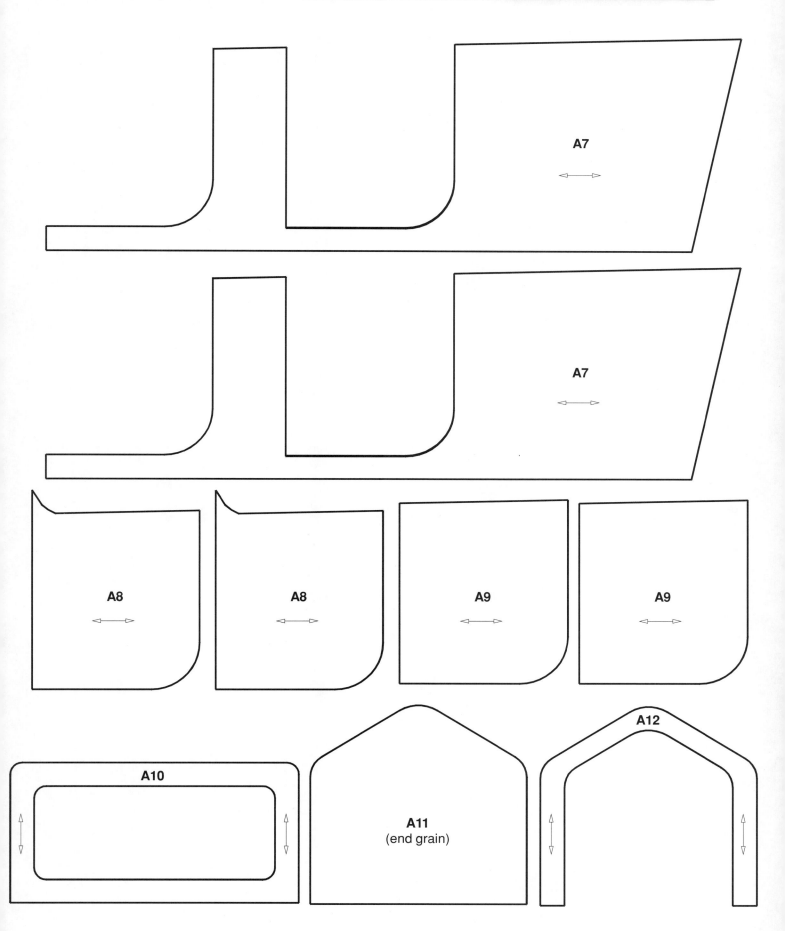

A7

A7

A8

A8

A9

A9

A10

A11
(end grain)

A12

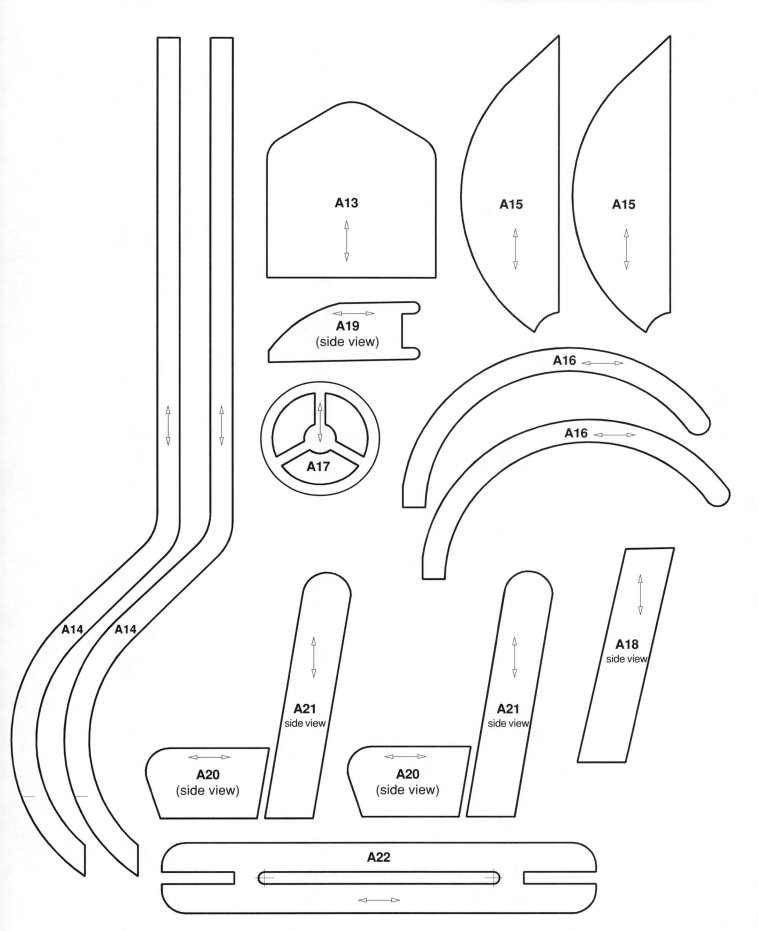

A13

A15

A15

A19
(side view)

A16

A16

A17

A14 **A14**

A18
side view

A21
side view

A21
side view

A20
(side view)

A20
(side view)

A22

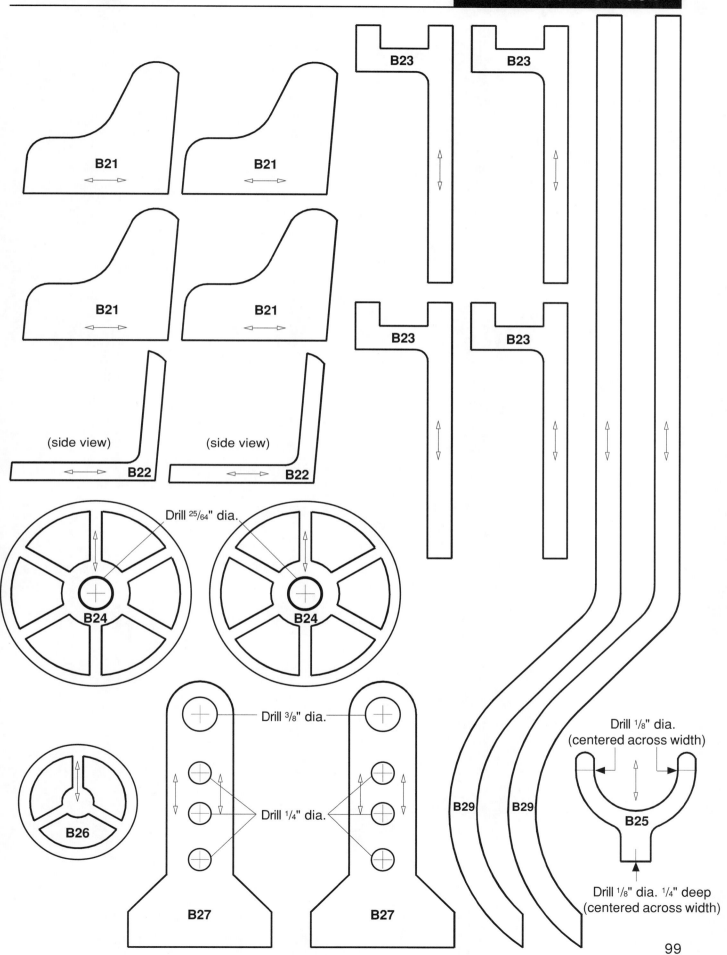

B23

B23

B21

B21

B23

B23

B21

B21

(side view)

(side view)

B22

B22

Drill 25/64" dia.

B24

B24

Drill 3/8" dia.

Drill 1/8" dia.
(centered across width)

B26

Drill 1/4" dia.

B29

B29

B25

B27

B27

Drill 1/8" dia. 1/4" deep
(centered across width)

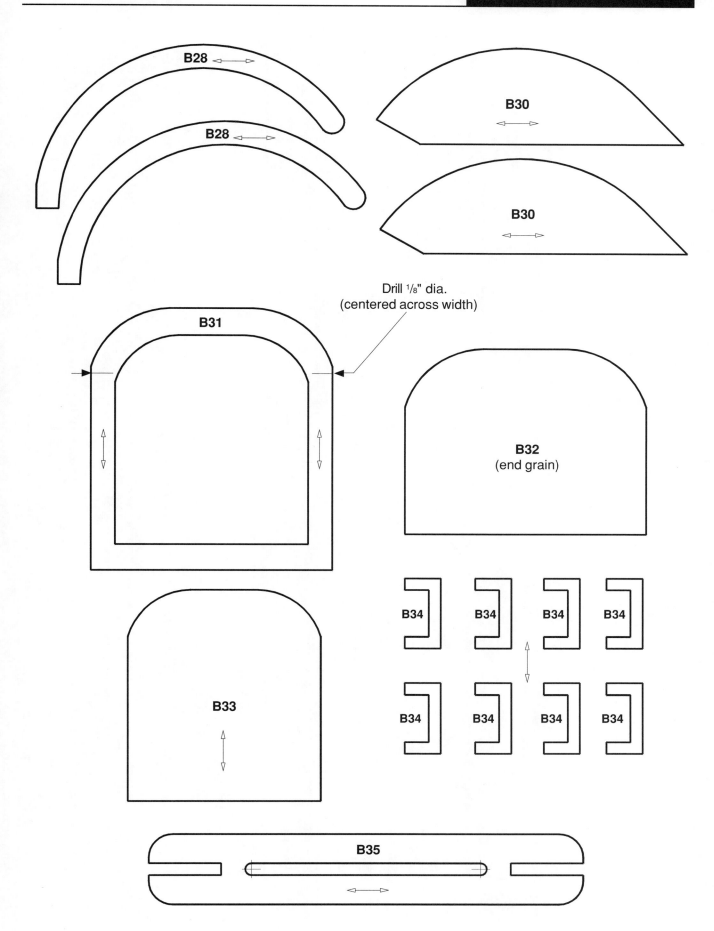

B28

B28

B30

B30

Drill ⅛" dia.
(centered across width)

B31

B32
(end grain)

B33

B34 B34 B34 B34

B34 B34 B34 B34

B35

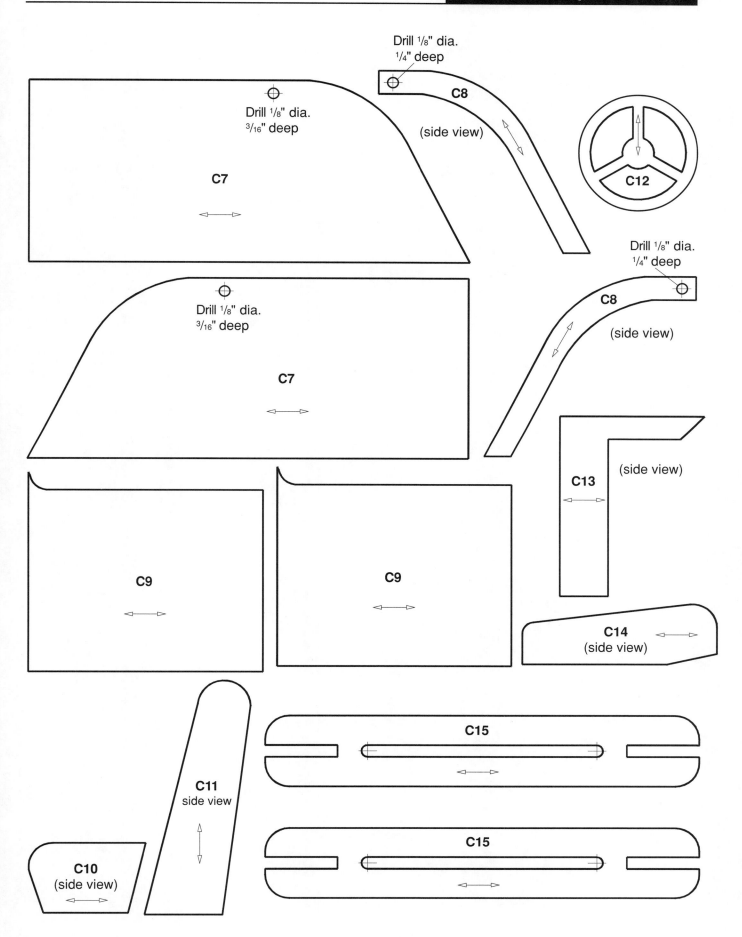

Drill 1/8" dia.
1/4" deep

C8

(side view)

Drill 1/8" dia.
3/16" deep

C7

C12

Drill 1/8" dia.
1/4" deep

C8

(side view)

Drill 1/8" dia.
3/16" deep

C7

C13

(side view)

C9

C9

C14
(side view)

C11
side view

C10
(side view)

C15

C15

Late-1920s Sport Sedan

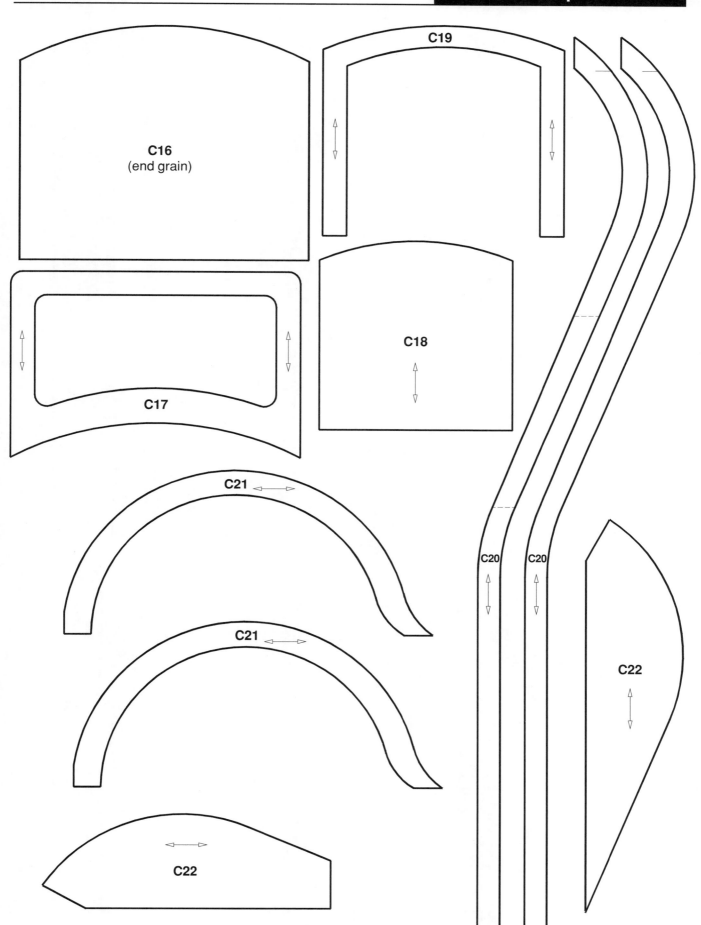

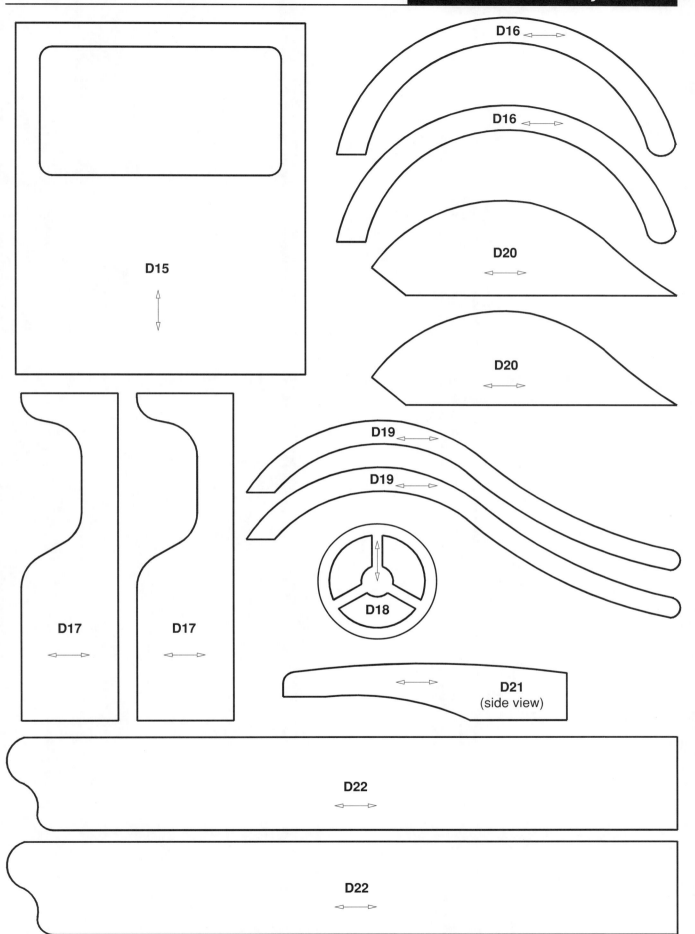

D16

D16

D20

D20

D15

D19

D19

D18

D17

D17

D21
(side view)

D22

D22

Late-1920s Delivery Truck

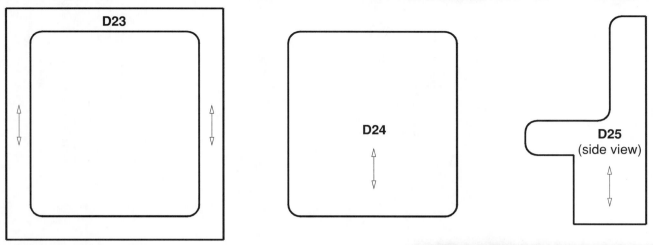

D23

D24

D25
(side view)

Late-1920s Town Sedan

E8

E8

E9

E9

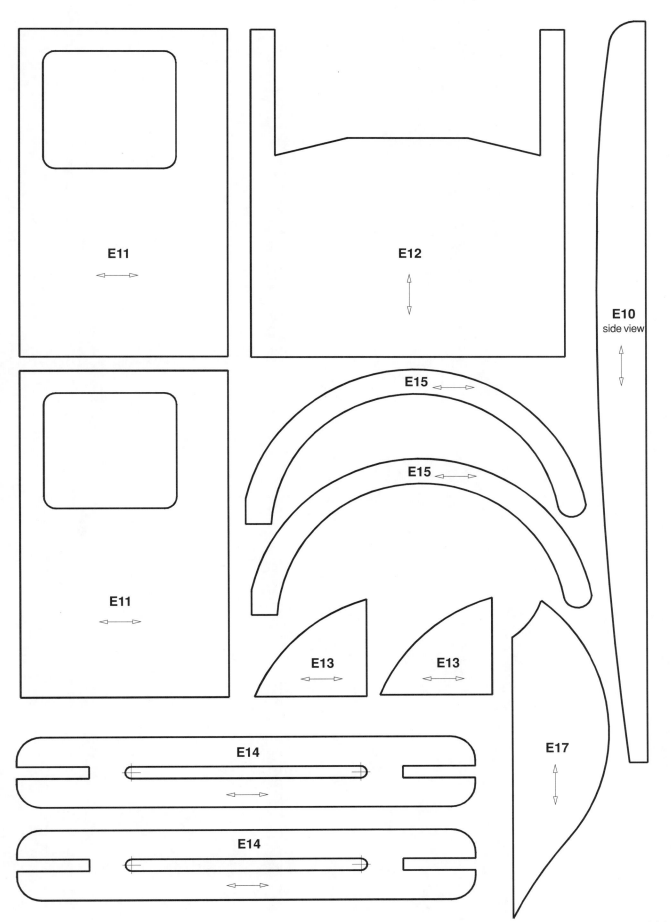

E11

E12

E10
side view

E11

E15

E15

E13

E13

E17

E14

E14

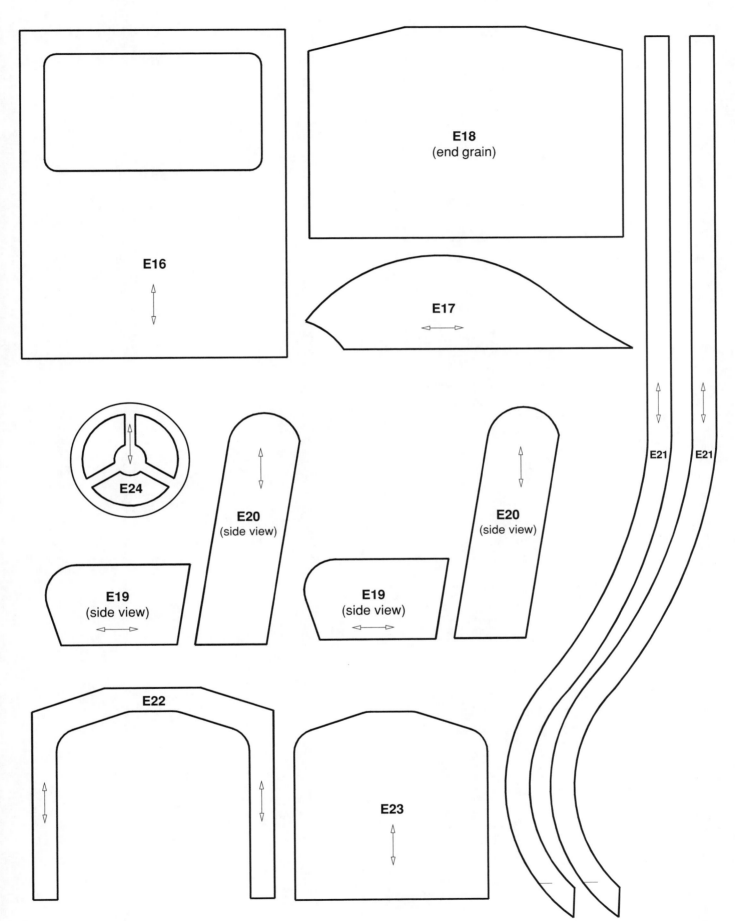

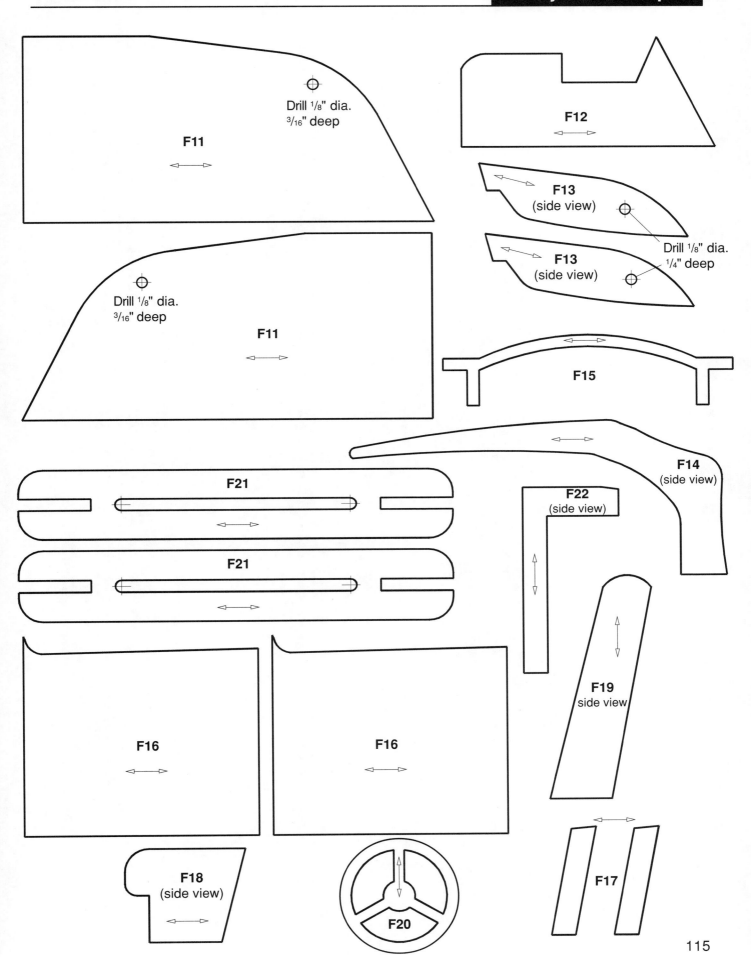

F11

Drill ⅛" dia.
³/₁₆" deep

F12

F13
(side view)

Drill ⅛" dia.
¼" deep

F13
(side view)

F11

Drill ⅛" dia.
³/₁₆" deep

F15

F14
(side view)

F21

F22
(side view)

F21

F19
side view

F16

F16

F18
(side view)

F20

F17

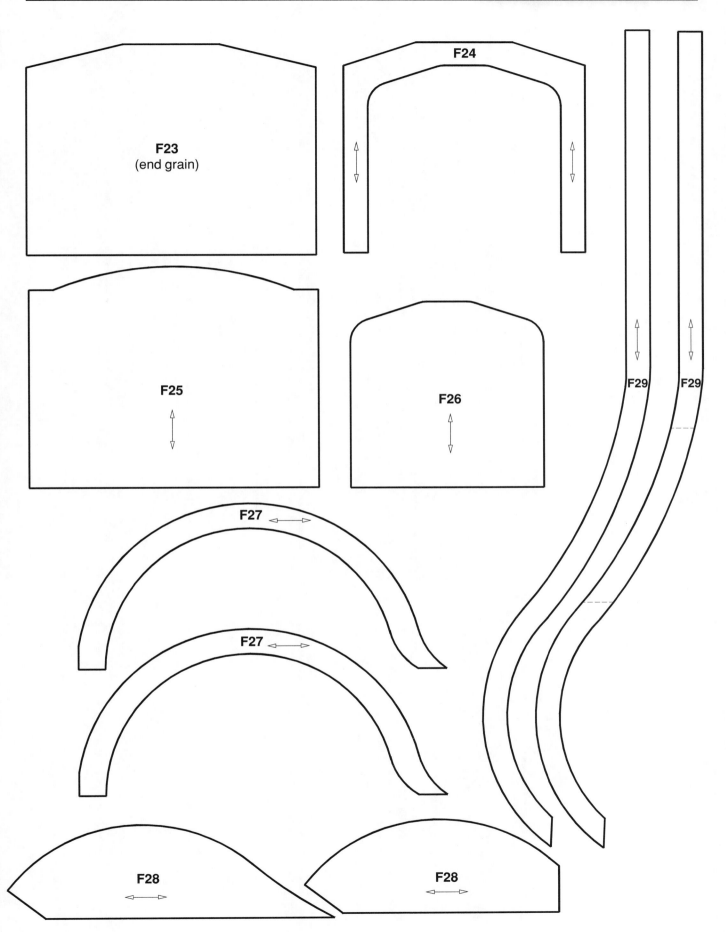

F23
(end grain)

F24

F25

F26

F27

F27

F28

F28

F29

F29

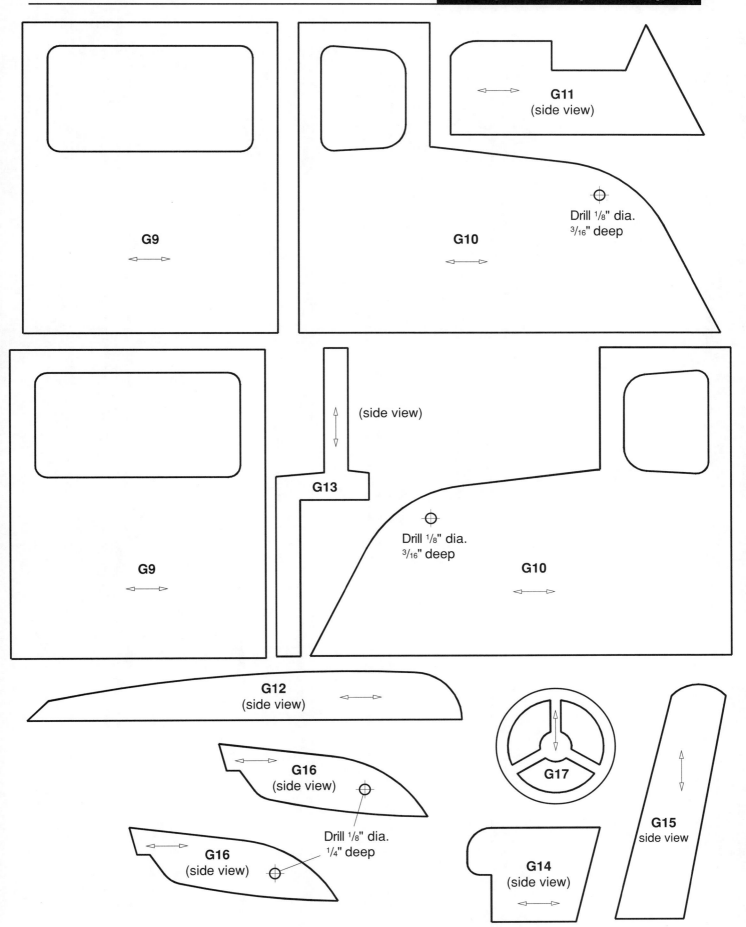

G9

G11
(side view)

G10

Drill 1/8" dia.
3/16" deep

G9

(side view)

G13

Drill 1/8" dia.
3/16" deep

G10

G12
(side view)

G16
(side view)

Drill 1/8" dia.
1/4" deep

G16
(side view)

G17

G15
side view

G14
(side view)

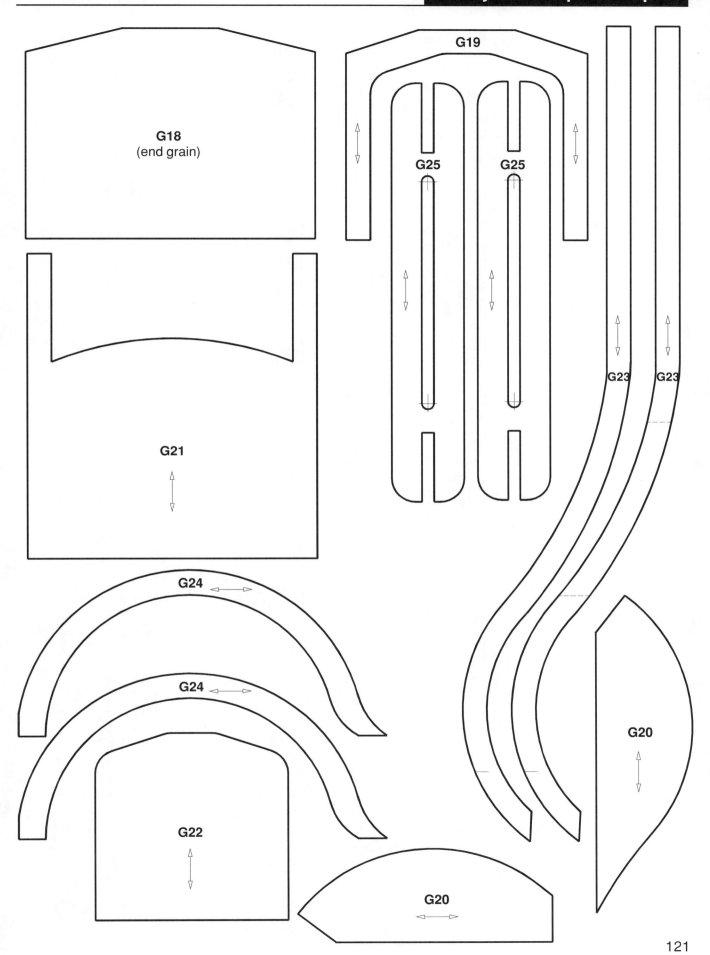

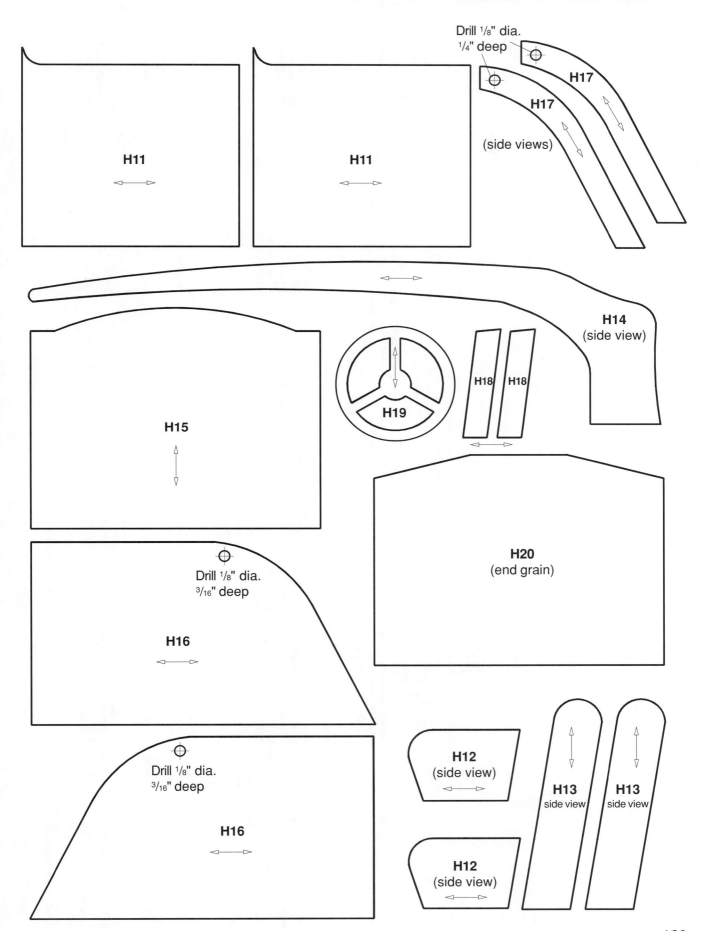

Drill ⅛" dia.
¼" deep

H17

H17

(side views)

H11

H11

H14
(side view)

H15

H18 **H18**

H19

H20
(end grain)

Drill ⅛" dia.
³/₁₆" deep

H16

Drill ⅛" dia.
³/₁₆" deep

H16

H12
(side view)

H13
side view

H13
side view

H12
(side view)

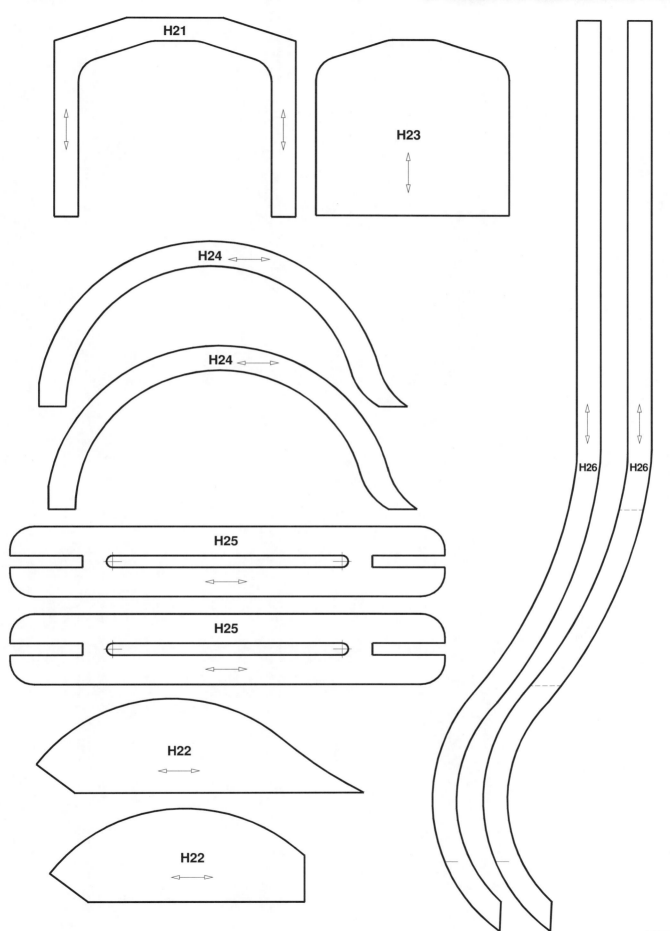

Other books available in the same collection

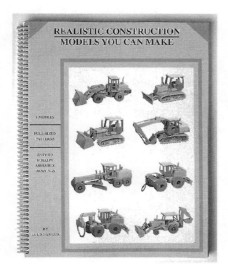

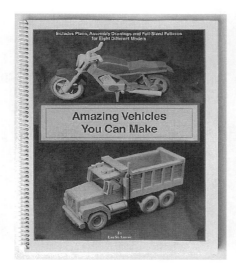

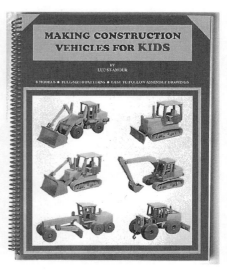

Realistic Construction Models You Can Make includes eight designs aimed at adults who want to build very realistic and detailed display models.

The models in this book have features such as movable pistons and cylinders, functional doors and other fine details.

If you enjoy precision and realism, this would be the right choice. This book includes two sets of full-sized patterns: one set is for reference to remain in the book; the second set is to stick onto the material for guidance in cutting. Step-by-step assembly drawings will guide you through to the finished product!

Amazing Vehicles You Can Make includes eight vehicles designed for both kids and adults. From a motorcycle to a train set, this book is sure to please you with a variety of different vehicles.

They are great as display models, with many fine details. Small parts added for detail that may not be suitable for young children are clearly marked on the plan (e.g. lights, mirrors, muffler and flashers).

Also includes two sets of full-sized patterns and step-by-step assembly drawings. If you are looking for great gift ideas, this book is sure to satisfy you.

Making Construction Vehicles For Kids includes eight vehicles with features kids love - levers that can be activated, parts that can be manipulated, etc.

Children will have hours of fun playing with these toys.

The eight models are the same as those found in *Realistic Construction Models You Can Make but* are larger. Plans are 25% bigger, so the models will stand the hard work that your little construction worker will put them through!
This book also includes two sets of full-sized patterns and step-by-step assembly drawings.

Contains the following models:

- Loader
- Dozer
- Dozer Loader
- Excavator
- Grader
- Skidder
- Grapple Skidder
- Backhoe

Contains the following models:

- Pick-up Truck
- Racing Car
- Motorcycle
- Airliner
- Train Set
- 18 Wheeler
- Dump Truck
- Cement Truck

Contains the following models:

- Loader
- Dozer
- Dozer Loader
- Excavator
- Grader
- Skidder
- Grapple Skidder
- Backhoe

ISBN: 1-896649-00-9
8 1/2 x 11 • 154 pages
Spiral Bound

ISBN: 1-896649-02-5
8 1/2 x 11 • 120 pages
Spiral Bound

ISBN: 1-896649-01-7
8 1/2 x 11 • 133 pages
Spiral Bound

See your nearest retailer to get a copy of these books.